# ASK THE SOUL DOCTOR

# ASK THE SOUL DOCTOR

*Holistic Solutions for Life's Toughest Challenges*

MARK PITSTICK MA, DC

Waterside Productions

Copyright © 2022 by Mark Pitstick

All rights reserved. No part of this book may be reproduced or transmitted in any form or by any means, electronic or mechanical, including photocopying, recording, or by any information storage or retrieval system without prior written permission from the author or his representatives.

Disclaimer: This book is to be regarded as a reference source and is not intended to replace professional medical advice or prescribe the use of any technique as a form of treatment for physical, emotional, or medical problems without the advice of your physician. The author and publisher disclaim any liability arising directly or indirectly from the use of this book.

Printed in the United States of America

First Printing, 2022

ISBN-13: 978-1-957807-57-7 print edition
ISBN-13: 978-1-957807-58-4 e-book edition

Waterside Productions
2055 Oxford Ave
Cardiff, CA 92007
www.waterside.com

# Endorsements for Dr. Pitstick's Other Books

**for *Soul Proof*...**

"Mark has summarized in a very readable fashion so much of the evidence for the afterlife. Congratulations on a masterful job!" – Ken Ring PhD

"Mark has assembled a wealth of evidence that can be immensely comforting and healing if you are open minded and ready to believe." – Bernie Siegel MD

"This unique book offers engaging evidence that we are eternal spiritual beings who exist before, during, and after our physical lives on earth." – Bill Guggenheim

**for *Radiant Wellness*...**

"A powerful approach to centering your life!" – Wayne Dyer EdD

"A sensible approach for the creation of a harmonious interaction between all the elements that structure your life." – Deepak Chopra MD

"I love your book, especially its spiritual context. Keep on writing and sharing!" – Elisabeth Kubler-Ross MD for *Greater Reality Living* (co-authored with Gary E. Schwartz PhD)

"Provides a host of practical recommendations to move to an unprecedented level of harmony and fulfillment here and now." – Eben Alexander MD

"I like their 'how-to' approach to integrating ideas about the afterlife with the practical realities of this life." – Raymond Moody MD, PhD

"The fear of total annihilation with physical death has probably caused more suffering in human history than all the physical diseases combined. Dr. Mark Pitstick and Dr. Gary Schwartz provide a potential 'cure' for this malady. – Larry Dossey MD

# Dedication

To my beloved family and friends on earth and beyond.

To Andy Lee, my dearest life partner, who provided valuable input based on her understandings as an evidential medium, RN, acupuncturist, and wise earth angel.

To the many people whose searching, struggling, and suffering motivated me to find meaningful answers to life's biggest questions and difficulties.

To my proofreaders Barbara Reed, Jennifer Horner, Leslie Klein, Chris Myers, Howie Abraham, and Alison Wakelin.

To the *15%ers* – intermediate and advanced beings whose evolved natures can greatly help others and make our world a better place.

To my higher-energy assistants – angels, guides, and master teachers – who love, support, guide, and remind me.

To E.L.G.O.D. – the Energizing, Loving, Guiding, Organizing, and Designing Presence and Power that created, sustains, and IS all life. My favorite names for Her include: Great Spirit, The Light, The Presence, All That Is, The Ground of All Being, One Mind, Life Source, Creator and Sustainer of All Life, Source Energy, Universal Intelligence, Creator, The One, The Divine, The Infinite, Higher Power, Infinite Intelligence, The Omniscient One, The Source.

To how peaceful, loving, joyful, and compassionate our world is becoming as more people awaken to *'The Great News'*.

# Table of Contents

Foreword . . . . . . . . . . . . . . . . . . . . . . . . . . . . . . . . . . . xi
Introduction . . . . . . . . . . . . . . . . . . . . . . . . . . . . . . . . . xv

Part One: Foundational Understandings . . . . . . . . . . . . . . . . . . . . 1
   1. Evidence of Afterlife . . . . . . . . . . . . . . . . . . . . . . . . . 3
   2. The Nature of Creator . . . . . . . . . . . . . . . . . . . . . . . . . 8
   3. The Nature of Material Persons / Humans . . . . . . . . . . . 15
   4. Higher-Energy Assistants / Assistance . . . . . . . . . . . . . 23
   5. The Nature of Reality . . . . . . . . . . . . . . . . . . . . . . . . 28
   6. 'Heaven' and 'Hell' . . . . . . . . . . . . . . . . . . . . . . . . . . 42
   7. 'the devil' and 'evil spirits' . . . . . . . . . . . . . . . . . . . . . 52
   8. Ghosts / Interim Postmaterial Persons . . . . . . . . . . . . . 56
   9. Enlightened Religious and Spiritual Teachings . . . . . . . 61
   10. The Greater Reality . . . . . . . . . . . . . . . . . . . . . . . . . 69
   11. The Afterlife . . . . . . . . . . . . . . . . . . . . . . . . . . . . . . 79
   12. Parallel Realities . . . . . . . . . . . . . . . . . . . . . . . . . . . 93
   13. After Death Communications . . . . . . . . . . . . . . . . . . . 99
   14. Evidential Mediums . . . . . . . . . . . . . . . . . . . . . . . . 107
   15. The SoulPhone Project . . . . . . . . . . . . . . . . . . . . . . 110

Part Two: Tough Challenges While on Earth . . . . . . . . . . . . . . . 117
   16. Why Would 'God' Allow ___? . . . . . . . . . . . . . . . . . . 119
   17. Optimal Grieving . . . . . . . . . . . . . . . . . . . . . . . . . . 126
   18. When a Child Changes Worlds . . . . . . . . . . . . . . . . 132
   19. When a Loved One Passes On . . . . . . . . . . . . . . . . 138
   20. When a Loved One's Body Dies by Suicide . . . . . . . 143

21. When a Pet Transitions to Next Phase of Life . . . . . . 153
22. When a Loved One's Physical Form Is Murdered . . . 159
23. When Your Body Is Dying . . . . . . . . . . . . . . . . . . . . 166
24. When Considering Suicide . . . . . . . . . . . . . . . . . . . .174
25. Optimally Handling Suffering . . . . . . . . . . . . . . . . . . 182

Part Three: Holistic Solutions . . . . . . . . . . . . . . . . . . . . . . . . 191
26. Fine-Tuning Your Body / Brain . . . . . . . . . . . . . . . . . 193
27. Communicating with 'Deceased' Loved Ones . . . . . . 200
28. Greater Reality Living . . . . . . . . . . . . . . . . . . . . . . . 212
29. Identify and Fulfill Your Purpose . . . . . . . . . . . . . . . 223
30. For More Evolved and Sensitive Persons . . . . . . . . . 230
31. Releasing Old Wounds, Fears, and Misinformation. . 240
32. Natural Health Care for Common Imbalances. . . . . . 250
33. Optimal Relationships for More Evolved People . . . . 257

Afterword . . . . . . . . . . . . . . . . . . . . . . . . . . . . . . . . . . . . . . 263
Glossary . . . . . . . . . . . . . . . . . . . . . . . . . . . . . . . . . . . . . . . 267
Resources . . . . . . . . . . . . . . . . . . . . . . . . . . . . . . . . . . . . . 283
About the Author . . . . . . . . . . . . . . . . . . . . . . . . . . . . . . . . 287

# Foreword
## by Gary E. Schwartz, PhD

> Years ago, I visited an old chapel with my four-year-old twin granddaughters. A large painting of 'God' hanging above the altar depicted a huge guy in the sky with long white hair and beard. We hadn't talked about the nature of Creator before since they were so young. They stared at it and then, unsolicited, one said with complete certainty: 'That's not what God looks like.' I said, *'Really. What do you think God looks like?'* She looked at me as though I was dense and should already know the answer to that question. *'A circle of light'*, she said. My other granddaughter nodded her head as though this were common knowledge.
> – Mark Pitstick

> *The important thing is not to stop questioning.*
> – Albert Einstein

Do you seek answers to some of life's most challenging and important questions, such as:

- Is there life beyond physical death?
- Is there a God / Creator / Universal Intelligence?
- Are angels, guides, and ghosts real?
- Do the minds / souls of animals, including our beloved pets, survive bodily death?

- Is it possible for people on earth to communicate with 'departed' beings?
- How can you release old wounds, fears, and misinformation?
- Are some mediums and channelers real?
- What happens to people who pass on by suicide?
- How can you identify and fulfill your purposes for being on earth?
- Why would a 'God' allow children to die, or people to do terrible things to others, animals, and the environment?
- How can you heal and evolve physically, psychologically, and spiritually?

Mark's *Ask the Soul Doctor* book provides state-of-the-art answers to these eleven big questions and many others. This is a book I have waited years to read. His analyses and syntheses are impressive.

I should confess at the outset that I am a fan of Dr. Pitstick. I have had the privilege to collaborate with him on the SoulPhone Project for more than five years. He spent most of his professional career as a clinician focusing on mind-body-spirit health. I spent most of mine as an academic professor and scientist focusing on psychophysiology, health psychology, energy medicine, and the emerging field of soul science.

Dr. Pitstick wrote, "I don't recall who first called me *'The Soul Doctor'* decades ago, but I am honored and do everything I can to deserve that title." Similarly, I do not remember who first called me *'The Soul Scientist'*. I, too, am honored and do my best to deserve that title. When a science-minded clinician (Dr. Pitstick) joins with a clinically-minded scientist (me) to address fundamental questions about life, the 'whole is greater than the sum of its parts.'

I decided to write this *Foreword* even though we don't yet have scientific evidence to validate all his answers. However, of all the books I know that address these profound questions, Mark's is the most comprehensive, thoughtful, inspiring, and evidence and experience based. Further, a long-term colleague and collaborator, Jennifer Horner, BSSE, MBA, independently concluded that *Ask the Soul Doctor* is among the best she has read in this area.

I am eager to see this book in print so I can gift it to family members, special colleagues, and those who contact me seeking advanced understanding about these foundational questions. I will also recommend it to college students who thirst for wisdom in this age of environmental destruction, COVID, war, political hostilities, and other challenges.

I hope that, someday, Dr. Pitstick's grandchildren will read this book and their souls will smile. May this book bring you much meaning, light, and peace.

Gary E. Schwartz, PhD
Professor of Psychology, Medicine, Neurology, Psychiatry and Surgery
Director, Laboratory for Advances in Consciousness and Health
Department of Psychology
The University of Arizona

# Introduction

Welcome and blessings to you! I hope the information in this book helps you – as it has me and many people – create a more happy, vital, and fulfilling earthly experience.

*We live in an exciting time in human history.* **Much evidence – from scientific research, clinical studies, and firsthand experiences – now clearly shows that life continues after bodily death.** This collective evidence is motivating more people to explore how to have an optimal experience now AND in the next realm. Contemporary understandings from this evidence make my answers and holistic solutions more credible and impactful.

Proof of afterlife and continuation of consciousness was **definitively demonstrated scientifically in 2020**. Based on the collective evidence, it can now be responsibly and accurately said that death of the earthly body is NOT the end of life. A resolute knowledge of this provides much hope, reassurance, and vision – especially during tough times.

Deeply knowing what I call *'The Great News'* is foundational to understanding my answers about life's biggest questions and challenges. I italicize these words and put them inside single quotation marks to help imprint them into your heart and mind. Please read this list daily until *it guides how you live while on earth*. Then share it and discuss with others so you understand this great news at an even higher level.

INTRODUCTION

## *'The Great News'*

The collective evidence indicates, with high degrees of certainty, that *you and everyone else:*

1. continue to live after bodily death, and may be living in parallel realities now.

2. do not really lose 'departed' loved ones and can interact with them again now.

3. are integral, infinite, eternal, and beloved parts of Source Energy / Creator.

4. receive assistance / guidance from angels, guides, master teachers, and evolved energies.

5. are sacredly interconnected with all people, animals, and nature.

6. have special purposes for being on this planet at this time.

7. have everything you need to survive and even thrive during this earthly adventure.

8. possess a magnificent body that, when cared for, can optimize your earthly experience.

9. can find meaning and trust the timing behind life's biggest changes such as death.

10. co-create how heavenly / hellish your life feels by your thoughts, words and deeds.

11. can find silver linings and opportunities for growth and service amidst challenges.

12. can likely use SoulPhone technology in the future for communication with postmaterial loved ones and luminaries who can help us heal our world.

**Knowing this great news helps you enjoy the many benefits of a greater reality living perspective and way of life.**

Before continuing, please read the following information found at the end of the book:

- **Read *About the Author*** since, given the significance of these questions, it's important to understand the training and experience behind my answers.

- **Read the *Glossary*** to better learn author's suggested terms included in my answers. That may sound boring, but it's essential. Words commonly used to discuss life, death, and afterlife may be relatively or totally inaccurate. *Updated terms can lead to a more informed discussion about the nature of reality.*

- **Review the *Resources*** to learn about free articles, radio shows, and newsletters at SoulProof.com. You will also get an overview of my books and audio programs with links to them. They are very affordable, especially considering the value of the information and strategies.

Note: This book was written while 'wearing the hats' of author, educator, holistic physician, counselor, and creator of Soul Proof outreaches. I did not write it as the director of the SoulPhone Foundation or research assistant for the SoulPhone Project. Those latter two roles would require that all my answers are based on solid scientific research. Except for #1 and 2 in *'The Great News'* (see below), that level of scientific certainty doesn't yet exist about other topics discussed in this book.

## Introduction

I don't recall who first called me '*The Soul Doctor*' decades ago, but I am honored and do everything I can to deserve that title. *That term does not imply that your essence needs saved.* What is needed is a holistic balance and communication between your body, brain, and higher consciousness. How to best live while on earth becomes clearer and easier when you remember who you are, why you are here, and Who walks beside you always.

The known physical universe and otherworldly realms are so vast and complex that I don't pretend to understand more than a fraction of it. **However, we have more information about the nature of reality than ever before in human history.** Greater glimpses and snippets can enlarge your view from, for example, a pinhole size to that of a silver dollar. A more expansive perspective makes such a difference for an optimal earthly experience.

My answers are based on my best current understandings from existing scientific research, clinical findings, my firsthand experiences, and those of others. My answers may change over time as I learn new information. My recommendations to discern your highest truth include:

1. sift through ancient religious / spiritual wisdom sources for kernels of truth.

2. learn contemporary evidence from scientific research and clinical data.

3. ask for assistance and discernment from E.L.G.O.D. and higher-energy assistants.

4. consider your firsthand experiences and those of others.

5. then decide / feel what makes the most sense to you.

***Again, please review the Glossary*** before reading my answers to commonly asked questions. Specific and accurate words are crucial for understanding the greater reality and enjoying this earthly experience. The words you read and say shape your thoughts. Your thoughts form your beliefs and those, in turn, greatly impact your actions.

For example, how much peace, joy, love, and fulfillment you feel is greatly affected by your worldview. Do you believe either #1 or 2 below?

1. Your life on this cruel planet is the result of random factors. Your earthly body is weak, and prone to sin and disease. When your body dies, you cease to exist. (Or, alternately, you might suffer in hell / enjoy heaven forever while many people live in torment.)

2. Your life on this incredible planet has meaning and purpose. Your body and brain are amazingly strong and resilient. When your body dies, 99% of who and what you really are continues to live in another realm. You shape the quality of that next phase of eternity.

Some people feel differently just reading those two very different perspectives. That's why I ask you to learn new words that have accurate meanings. It's well worth the time and effort.

## Notes...

1. My answers to questions are divided into three parts: (a) *Foundational Understandings*, (b) *Tough Challenges While on Earth*, and (c) *Holistic Solutions*

2. To maintain confidentiality, the names of the persons asking questions are not given. For the same reason, distinguishing details – such as the name, date and manner of bodily death of a loved one – were changed or removed.

## Introduction

3. The articles, books, and audio products listed at the beginning of each Question Section are recommended for that topic. See *Resources* at the end of this book for more information about them. Additional suggestions may be included in my answers.

4. I am honored by the implied trust when people share their most difficult struggles and questions with me. It is a sacred privilege to assist people during their darkest hours. But I won't say that as I answer each question.

5. Although I am very sorry for the pain and suffering that most questioners experience, I will not say that repetitively in my answers. Similarly, I send prayers, blessings, best wishes, and healing energies to all those who suffer, but also won't mention that with every answer.

6. If all the *light, energy, and information* – the most fundamental components of life – that exist in our world were the size of Mt. Everest, the portion detected by the average person would be the size of a golf ball. Based upon estimates by top physicists from around the world, this comparison was reported by science journalist Lynne McTaggart in *The Field*. That and other scientific estimates form the basis for my statements that the average person senses much less than 1% of reality. Likewise, estimates are that much less than 1% of who and what a person is really perishes when the earthly body dies.

7. Some questions are so 'big' that understanding other parts of this book is required to fully address them. You may have to use recommended resources and 'chew on' my answers for a while before comprehending, healing, and transforming.

8. I'll use multiple words separated by a forward slash for more accurate meanings. Examples are: person / soul, and multilocation / parallel realities / simultaneous experiences.

9. I will mainly use feminine pronouns 'she' and 'her' since 'he' and 'him' were used excessively in the past. I'll use single instead of double quotation marks to denote my paraphrase of older quotes that used 'man' instead of 'people'.

10. Because of my early religious upbringing and theological training, I am most knowledgeable about Protestant Christianity. I have learned and benefited much from other denominations and religions, but my early training will show through. I am very respectful of and grateful for different views that provide meta-understandings of Creator, life, and afterlife.

11. I purposely repeat certain themes and acknowledge that may seem overly so. However, this repetition can reverse misinformation that has been widely taught and believed for many years.

12. My answers may sound glib or even callous if you are in the middle of tough challenges. However, they may make more sense while remembering who you are, why you are here, what you are capable of, and your interconnection with Source.

Basically, how you respond to any adversity primarily depends on two factors: (a) Do you believe you are a powerless victim of cruel chance? or (b) Do you know you are a powerful being of energy / consciousness who is an integral, expanding, and beloved part of Life right now and always? Learning new terms and remembering all this takes a bit of work. But it's very worthwhile for those who want to learn sensible answers to life's biggest questions and challenges.

*Article #s listed for further information can be found at SoulProof.com/Articles.*

# Part 1: Foundational Understandings

# QUESTION SECTION #1: EVIDENCE OF AFTERLIFE

Three categories of afterlife evidence clearly show that life continues after the human form perishes. These include evidence from scientific research, clinical studies, and firsthand experiences. Taken together, this is termed **the collective evidence** for life after death.

**Scientific research** has definitively shown that life continues after bodily death. This category of evidence includes findings from experiments performed by scientists in a university or institute laboratory. The following criteria are required for research to be considered truly scientific: replicated, double-blinded, controlled, multi-centered, and random-ordered experiments with highly statistically significant findings published in peer-reviewed scientific journals. To date, this research includes university-based experiments on evidential mediums and communication with postmaterial (so-called 'deceased') persons.

**Clinical studies** also clearly indicate the survival of consciousness after death. This category of evidence involves data collected and analyzed by university professors, physicians, and / or psychologists in professional offices and hospitals. Types of clinical studies include: near death experiences, past life memories / regressions, perinatal experiences, Life Between Lives(R) sessions, shared crossings, terminal lucidity cases, and deathbed visions.

***Firsthand experiences*** are personal perceptions that have been reported by many people in different cultures over time. These *direct experiences* add to the collective evidence for the continuation of life after death. This category of evidence is the least objective, but often the most personally meaningful. Firsthand perceptions pass the *seeing is believing* or, more accurately, *sensing is believing* test. Types of firsthand experiences include: after death communications, out of body experiences, ghost sightings, spiritually transformative experiences, electronic voice projection / instrumental transcommunication, and other ways of knowing.

Past generations had to rely on faith and religious teachings about an afterlife. That is sufficient for some people, especially when not faced with tough challenges. However, **knowing the collective evidence can more deeply assure you – even in the darkest of times – that death is NOT the end of life.** The more you internalize that great news, the more you can *live as though you are immortal ... because you are.*

## **Articles** (again, all articles found at SoulProof.com/Articles)

*#1 Scientific Evidence That Bodily Death Is NOT the End of Life*

*#28 After Death Communications*

*#35 The SoulPhone*

*#60 Clinical Evidence That Life Continues After Physical Death*

*#94 Near Death Experiences*

*#95 Death Bed Visions*

*#96 Shared Crossings*

*#97 Terminal Lucidity*

*#98 Life Between Lives Sessions*

*#99 Perinatal Experiences*

**Books** (learn more about books in *Resources* at the end of this book)

*The Afterlife Evidence, Soul Proof, Greater Reality Living*

**Q#1: How do you really know there is life after death? This is such an important question. What if you are wrong?**

A#1: Thank you for verbalizing what MANY people on our planet fear. I agree that this is one of the most important questions to be asked. I have researched the topic of life after death for 50 years since working with many suffering and dying people and their families in hospitals. Seeing the bodies of children die especially motivated me to find evidence-based answers to the question *'Is there really life after death?'* That was a pivotal question before addressing others such as 'Why are we here? Why do children die? How can God allow so much suffering?' and others.

Each decade, my degree of certainty about life after death increased. The largest jump occurred during the last six years while working with Gary E. Schwartz PhD. A former assistant professor at Harvard and tenured professor at Yale, he is a senior professor at the University of Arizona. Dr. Schwartz directs the *Laboratory for Advances in Consciousness and Health* where research on the SoulPhone Project is conducted. In our book *Greater Reality Living*, he stated: **"Speaking as a scientist, I am now 99.9 percent certain that life continues after the human body dies."**

That is a super high degree of certainty for a reputable scientist to claim. He could only state that after many years of solid scientific research. Our combined deep knowledge of the clinical data and firsthand experience evidence strengthened that certainty. To learn more about this evidence, read the articles listed above.

Emerging postmaterial communication technology should remove much or all fear and doubt about life after death. Read article #35 and subscribe to the free newsletter at SoulPhone.comto receive updates about this project.

**Q#2: If there really is life after death, why do scientists usually not believe in it?**

A#2: Scientists make conclusions based on replicated research and findings published in peer-reviewed journals. Until 2020, that didn't exist for this area of research. In addition, many scientists and university professors are atheists or agnostics. As such, they operate with *a preconceived mindset* that life ends when the body and brain die. Why would they be interested in trying to prove something that, in their belief system, doesn't exist? Another factor is concern about funding and standing within a university. Scientists who investigate survival of consciousness risk loss of funding for existing projects. Further, they could lose their department status and even their jobs. That's a big deal for academics and university professors.

Finally, *a cold war has existed between science and religion over the last several centuries.* Just five hundred years ago, it was widely believed by religious leaders and other prominent thinkers that the sun revolved around the earth. Using the newly invented telescope, Galileo discovered that the earth revolves around the sun. He was found guilty of heresy and subjected to house arrest until his death. Perhaps church officials feared that focusing on science versus faith would uncover other unsubstantiated religious teachings.

For all these reasons, *it's understandable that scientists today are hesitant to investigate a topic that has largely been the domain of religion.*

Open-minded scientists who follow the data will be challenged when the scientific findings of Dr. Schwartz and others are officially announced and demonstrated. Will skeptics trust the scientific method even if it shows their personal beliefs about no life after death are wrong? Read Dr. Schwartz's book *Extraordinary Claims Require Extraordinary Evidence* to learn more about this exciting time in history and the importance of accurately discerning fact from fiction.

**Q#3: I've seen articles on the internet and heard blogs that there really isn't life after death. They say it's a hoax that anything continues after the body dies. What do you think?**

A#3: The wonderful thing about knowing the collective evidence is that *it doesn't matter what I think*. What matters are conclusions based on the preponderance of evidence. Attention to evidence and facts don't matter to some people these days, but *labelling something as 'fake' doesn't make it so.*

Many scientists, physicians, and psychologists are members of the Academy for Advances in Postmaterialist Science. They agree that much evidence indicates **consciousness is primary, not a temporary phenomenon that perishes when the earthly body does.** To learn more about this visionary group of open-minded skeptics, visit AAPSGlobal.com.

I encourage you to read the articles and books listed above and make your own informed conclusions.

# QUESTION SECTION #2: THE NATURE OF CREATOR

Understanding the nature of the Creator and Sustainer of All Life is an ultra-important key to handling the biggest challenges on earth. Difficulties look even more bleak if you believe that a mercurial cosmic dictator arbitrarily decides when and how people suffer and die. That model about the nature of The Divine instills blind allegiance in some people, but fear and confusion in many others. Erroneous teachings about Source Energy have caused many people to reject any notion of a Higher Power, afterlife, and meaning to existence.

**The One is pure peace, love, creativity, wisdom, light, and much more.** *And you are an integral, infinite, eternal, and beloved part of That One.* Some religious denominations have done a very poor job of teaching that we each are one with the Ground of All Being. Becoming part of Source Energy is not something you have to achieve; it is how life is set up. As Eastern Indian spiritual teacher Meher Baba said, "To attain union with God is so impossibly difficult because it is impossible to become what you already are!"

Years ago, I visited an old chapel with my four-year-old twin granddaughters. A large painting of 'God' hanging above the altar depicted a huge guy in the sky with long white hair and beard. We hadn't talked about the nature of Creator before since they were so young. They stared at it and then one said with complete certainty:

'That's not what God looks like.' I said, 'Really. What do you think God looks like?' She looked at me as though I was dense and should already know the answer. **'A circle of light'**, she said. The other nodded her head as though this were common knowledge.

Expanding your understandings about The Light / The Presence can expand your peace, joy, love, gratitude, compassion, enthusiasm, and enlightenment.

Fear-based characteristics attributed to a huge male deity (He and Him) instantly seem ludicrous when using female pronouns (She and Her). I use male pronouns when referring to archaic and erroneous depictions of 'God'. By contrast, I use female pronouns for more sensible and contemporary understandings. In addition, I use the impersonal pronoun 'It' sometimes to remind us that One Mind is beyond gender.

## Articles
*#13 What is E.L.G.O.D. Really Like?*

*#78 Why Did God Take My Loved One?*

*#83 Am I a Christian?*

**Books:** *The Eleven Questions, Soul Proof, The Big Picture of Life*

**Audio Programs**: (learn more about books in *Resources* at the end of this book)

*Ask Your Soul, G.O.D. and Angels*

### Q#1: Where did Creator come from?

A#1: *That's considered an unknowable question.* It's like asking how, when, and where life or consciousness started. Mind-blowing

## The Nature of Creator

to think about that for very long, isn't it? The best answer I can share is that **this level of power, intelligence, love, and creativity always existed**. Astrophysicists describe a Big Bang that ultimately led to the formation of earth and the known physical universe. *But when and from where did that energy and potential arise?* Perhaps we will understand such things in the future as SoulPhone technology enables communication with postmaterial persons, angels / guides / master teachers, and One Mind.

### Q#2: How did a supposedly loving God get portrayed as such a fearful fellow?

A#2: One answer is because so many people are fearful. The 'God' that emerged in their thinking and writing reflected, in part, the fear and vengeance from that mass consciousness.

Your word 'fellow' is another key to my answer. Replace 'fellow' (He) with 'woman' (She) and the various horrors attributed to Life Source sound ludicrous. Unless referring to mistaken images of 'God', I will use the feminine pronouns She and Her to correct misunderstandings perpetuated by patriarchal cultures / religions about Creator. A partial list of bizarre teachings about The Infinite One are that 'He':

a. created people, then quickly judged them as hopeless sinners

b. created floods, pestilence, etc. to destroy those recently considered to be 'very good'

c. tested Job by destroying all he had

d. tested Abraham by ordering him to kill his son Isaac

e. allowed a formidable evil, red-skinned, horned being to influence and hurt His children

f. required that His only son suffered and died so He could give people another chance

The list of strange, especially if taken literally, teachings goes on and on. These are particularly shocking for people who think for themselves and listen to their inner voice. The Beloved could never imagine such strange actions, but people who altered sacred texts could.

Many adults have shared with me how shocked they were as children to hear such stories about a God who was supposedly loving and wise. They listened to their hearts and found different churches with teachings more in line with how a loving parent would act. People who remain in fundamentalist sects somehow justify such cruel and dictatorial behavior by 'God'. Some people have shared with me their inner struggles about such strange teachings. Then they felt guilty for doubting 'God' and fear *He might turn on them*. Relationships with a 'God' like that are more fearful and fawning than loving and trusting.

**Believing schizoid notions about 'God' is one reason things on earth are so bad.** *After all, if 'God' can torture and kill those who look, act, and believe differently, then why can't people do the same?* This line of thinking is justifiable for those who believe they are on 'the one true path'.

Rediscovering *original meanings* of sacred teachings conveys greatly different views. Aramaic translations, for example, reveal more accurate understandings from pivotal times and places that so greatly influenced Judaism, Islam and Christianity.

Regarding Aramaic meanings, Neil Douglas-Klotz PhD stated on my radio show *Soul-utions*: "The root words for God are '*Eloha*' or '*Alaha*' from the Hebrew '*Elohim*.' All these words mean 'unity, sacred unity, or one Beingness'. The Jewish or Aramaic notion of The Divine is not a being sitting somewhere, someplace as in a room above us, but a unity of which we are a part."

## The Nature of Creator

He continued, "Both Jesus and Hebrew prophets before him shared this bigger picture of the Divine. That's quite different from our Western conception. The problem is that, when this conception was squeezed through the Greek language and thinking into Western Christianity, only a very small part of this meaning was carried across the language bridge."

Nonsensical teachings about Creator also arose when 'religious leaders' and powerful rulers conspired to twist early teachings into fearful messages. This strategy was successful in controlling some people who donated money they didn't have for building huge churches and lavish lifestyles for the elite. But it kept many people from wanting anything to do with such a 'God'. Some people became atheists because they found that to be more comforting and credible than believing in Him.

If your early teachings about The Divine seemed strange to you, realize you were right. The offending information was incomplete or **just plain wrong**. I hope you listened to your inner knowing about how a loving and caring Higher Power would operate. If you haven't, it's not too late to establish a personal and loving relationship.

The following description of Creator is more consistent with contemporary evidence. In *Destiny of Souls*, Michael Newton PhD, quoted a very evolved client's description of The One during a *Life Between Lives* session. She described The Presence as: *'Massive but soft. Powerful yet gentle. There is a breath, a whisper of sound that is so pure. The sound creates all, including light and energy. The sound holds this structure and makes it move, shifting and undulating, creating everything. It is a reverberating bell, then a high-pitched pure humming like an echo of a mother full of love singing to her child.'*

I hope this discussion helps answer your very important question.

**Q#3: How can I develop a better relationship with Creator? My early fundamentalist Christian experiences turned me away from Him. But now I've learned more sensible descriptions and want to renew that connection.**

A#3: Excellent decision! Two of the best ways are to pray and meditate. Daily ask to renew your connection from your heart of hearts, but remember that your prayers aren't designed to get Creator's attention or sway Her decisions. They are to remind you that – just like the poem *Footprints in the Sand* – the Omniscient One always walks with you. As Lord Alfred Tennyson wrote in his poem *The Higher Pantheism:* "Speak to Him, thou, for He hears, and Spirit with Spirit can meet. Closer is He than breathing, and nearer than hands and feet."

A statement attributed to the great Eastern Indian teacher Kabir is instructive. When asked by students about how to know The Infinite One, Kabir answered: 'Path presupposes distance. If He be near, no path needs thou at all. Verily, it makes me smile to hear of a fish in water that is thirsty!'

In other words, E.L.G.O.D. is all and is in all. And, **great news alert**, we each are important parts of Her just as a huge tapestry consists of many threads. Asking The Presence for a renewed relationship is akin to inviting your higher self to come to the fore in your life; it's already there. Your task is to remember that each moment and live with the peace, joy, love, and meaning that naturally flows.

*A big part of my life these days revolves around remembering who I am and Who walks beside me always.* My list for realizing that as much as possible includes prayer, meditation, yoga, time in nature, serving others, loving relationships, optimal self-care, and using the information and resources shared in this book. This has helped me KNOW that **we each are one with The One and sacredly** *interconnected with all life.* In addition to articles listed above, I also recommend #11, 12, 16, 17, 20, 21, 51, and 89.

### Q#4: Do humans provide 'experience and data feedback' for the evolvement of Universal Intelligence?

A#4: Absolutely! I love how you stated this and heartily agree. Source Energy can infinitely evolve and expand, just like you and me; It is not static and fully formed. Archaic models of a big guy in the sky presumed that 'God' was a finished and perfect product. In that view, material persons are weak and ignorant sinners who need direction and help from this powerful patriarchal ruler.

*More accurate depictions of The Infinite are that of an ever-expanding phenomenon.* I envision this as like **a cosmic amoeba of energy / light / intelligence** that continually grows and refines. Like an amoeba, its pseudopods extend outwardly to explore new horizons. Newly collected information is sent back to The Source. It's an inspiring way to view how life unfolds.

*Where there's a why, there's a way.* The above model means that even your supposed failures benefit others via positive ripples and stored info-energy. Knowing that your earthly experiences can be meaningful — even when they don't seem like it — gives you more hope and motivation to do your very best. You are not alone in the quest to help others and our world. It is happening right now as more *15%ers* awaken and take action.

# QUESTION SECTION #3: THE NATURE OF MATERIAL PERSONS / HUMANS

Some questions I receive are *based on inaccurate beliefs* that people:
- are mere physical beings who cease to exist after bodily death
- are separate from Source
- can lose their loved ones
- are relatively weak
- might suffer in eternity forever

These inaccurate beliefs, in turn, *result in questions and statements with false suppositions*:
- What if my life ends when I die?
- I can't handle being on earth anymore.
- Why did God take my loved one?
- I lost my mother last month.

- Will God judge me for questioning Him?

I'm not criticizing these beliefs, questions, or statements. Nor am I minimizing the pain and suffering behind them. **However, inaccurate beliefs — and accompanying words — create needless misunderstandings and fears.** And those, in turn, engender lower-energy thoughts and actions. That's why it's so important to seek accurate and evidence-based answers to one of life's biggest questions: 'Who am I?" Or, to put it another way, 'What is the nature of material persons?'

## Articles
*#11 Expanding Your View of Life*

*#15 The Nature of Humans / Material Persons*

*#56 Are You "The Weird One" In Your Family?*

*#68 The Big Picture of Life*

**Books:** *Soul Proof, The Big Picture of Life*

**Audio Programs**: *Ask Your Soul, G. O.D. and Angels*

### Q#1: What is your answer to the big 'Who am I?' question?

A#1: You are a unique and deathless being of energy / awareness who can manifest in different ways, times, and places. You are a WISP — a Wise, Infinite, Special, and Powerful part of life. You may *seem* like a frail physical person who dies after a relatively short life. But this earthly experience is just a tiny fraction of your eternal life.

During my early twenties, music was a great help in remembering my true nature. Sometimes just the names of songs were very instructive. One example by the band *Yes* was *We Have Heaven* — a concise and accurate description of reality when you are awakened to your real nature. Another by the same group was *Perpetual Change*, a beautiful description of life as never ending but often changing.

Words and melodies were like mantras that played over and over in my head. They provided clues as I searched for meaningful answers to life's biggest questions. I am grateful to the musicians who helped me recover from spiritual amnesia. A few examples:

1. *Shining Star* by Earth, Wind, and Fire: "You're a shining star, no matter who you are, shining bright to see what you could truly be."

2. *The End* by The Beatles: "And in the end, the love you take is equal to the love you make."

3. *Deja Vu* by CSN&Y: "If I had ever been here before, I would probably know just what to do. (Then a different voice that asks…) Don't you?"

4. *Higher Ground* by Stevie Wonder: "I'm so glad that He let me try it again, cause my last time on earth I lived a whole world of sin. I'm so glad that I know more than I knew then. Gonna keep on tryin' till I reach my highest ground."

5. *Music* by Cat Stevens: "Think about the light in your eyes, think about what you should know. There'd be no wars in the world if everybody joined in the show."

6. *Within You Without You* by The Beatles: "When you've seen beyond yourself, then you may find peace of mind is waiting there. And the time will come when you'll see we're all one, and life flows on within you and without you.

Those are some of my answers to your question 'Who am I?' However, *your answers* are the ones that matter the most for you.

## The Nature of Material Persons / Humans

I hope the information and resources in this book will help you find meaningful ones that assist an optimal earthly experience.

**Q#2: I don't understand why people come to a place like earth. What is the point if we are all one and part of the same incredible Force?**

A#2: To learn lessons. Most people — including myself — don't fully *know and show* they are one with Source Energy and sacredly interconnected with all life. This earthly experience can help us learn and demonstrate that more deeply.

Why weren't we created completely knowing this? If, upon arriving on earth, you automatically and fully remembered your real nature, you would be a pre-programmed robot. Put another way, if you were created completely aware of and in alignment with good / E.L.G.O.D., you would be an automaton, and Creator would be a cosmic puppet master.

*You also couldn't learn and grow from lessons borne from searching and struggling.* It's easy to remember who you are and live accordingly when in sublime realms where higher energies abound. Deep realization and internalized knowing are heightened after experiencing the blood, sweat, and tears involved in an earthly visit. Consider difficult lessons you learned as a child. For example, your parents warned you to not touch something hot, but their words were meaningless until you experienced what hot is.

Similarly, how can you freely choose love, peace, joy, compassion, and other higher-energy emotions and ways of being until you've experienced their opposites?

Visiting earth is a great way to awaken. If you are suffering, you are more likely to ask key questions that you wouldn't have if everything were perfect. If you are a beginner soul, manifesting part of your life force on earth provides opportunities to have spiritually transformative experiences. If you are an intermediate or advanced person, this earthly experience can help you evolve further, serve others, and enjoy unique adventures and pleasures.

This earthly incarnation is a voluntary experience that helps you evaluate and demonstrate how much you really understand. Again, it's easier to learn lofty ideas in a safe and totally supportive nonearthly environment. **The real test** — where the rubber really meets the road — is during earthly experiences where it *appears* you are separate, weak, vulnerable, and can die.

### Q#3: *How can I work with suffering people without taking on their painful energy?*

A#3: Learn how to shield yourself. Being able to help others without paying for it emotionally and / or physically can be a bit of a balancing act. It's best done one moment and one person at a time. I've served many suffering people for fifty years and learned how to not take on their lower energies.

One key to doing that involves understanding *the nature of material persons*. Although people appear to be solid, they really are mostly empty space with high energy particles whirling around. You and everyone else are comprised of *energy and information*. Clinical and scientific terms for this are mind, consciousness, and awareness. More religious terms are soul or spirit. That's who you and everyone else really are.

*Info-energy* can manifest in higher, positive, and more refined ways. Thoughts, words, and actions of people on this wavelength predominately focus on peace, joy, compassion, love, gratitude, enthusiasm, and enlightenment.

## The Nature of Material Persons / Humans

However, info-energy can manifest in lower, negative, and grosser ways. People who operate more at this level experience lower-energy emotions and ways of being such as anger, fear, grief, hopelessness, guilt, and shame. Less evolved and less aware people may sap / drain or zap / attack others without being aware of it. They deserve love and compassion, but must learn that they should not hurt others. They need patient teaching and care as they learn *self-responsibility*. It's both difficult and freeing to know that we create the quality of our lives.

This view of the nature of people can help you make an important distinction: *everyone is doing the best* **they think they can** *given their current level of consciousness, information, and resources.* When people know better, they do better. Beginner souls and imbalanced people who act inappropriately often were abused and / or taught limiting and erroneous information. They were often wounded, misinformed, and stuck in those lower-energy ways of being. But all that is reversible.

Some people are overwhelmed by life's changes and need temporary help to dig out. Just today, I received an email from a woman with six close family and friends who changed worlds in three months. People like her want to change but need more information, support, and resources to do so.

Unfortunately, I've found that only 1 in 10 people really want to work on themselves. Many aren't really ready to improve themselves. As soon as they get relief of their worst pain, whether physical or emotional, they stop treatment and self-care. They may feel that they get more 'secondary gains' by talking about how bad they have it than taking their life to a higher level. No judgment or criticism, it's just the way many people are.

To protect yourself from people who are *stuck in lower-energy emotions*, try the following:

a. Maintain distance from them whenever possible.

b. Cross your arms over your chest to shield your energetic heart.

c. Wash your hands with cold water as soon as possible after interacting with them.

d. Shake your hands briskly as if throwing water off them.

e. Use the 'Lion's Breath' technique (see YouTube searches) and breathe deeply.

Do all you can to diminish suffering and ignorance / misinformation. But remember that much of what your brain reports about reality is wrong. Don't bring your work home or get too involved in the trauma-drama. Remember the big picture of life and take time to enjoy the journey and wonderful parts of life.

The task for healers and teachers is to live with one foot on earth and the other in higher realms. Doing this as impeccably as possible is considered a *shaman's / master's path* to higher service, growth, and enlightenment.

Working with those who are suffering invites you to achieve this seemingly impossible task: keep an open heart and do everything possible to relieve suffering AND, *at the same time*, maintain compassion and remember the big picture of life. The following messages have been very helpful for me:

- Ram Dass: To become a more awakened divine-human: Love, Serve, Remember.

- Sri Chinmoy (from his poem *Revelation*): "No more my heart shall sob or grieve. My days and nights dissolve in God's

## The Nature of Material Persons / Humans

own Light. Above the toil of life, my soul is a Bird of Fire winging the Infinite."

- Buddhism: Do what you feel called to do, but don't be attached to the outcome.

- Esther Hicks who channels a higher collective consciousness called Abraham: 'Don't take score too soon.' From a limited earthly perspective, you can't fully gauge what game you are playing, let alone know if you are winning or not. *Reach for the highest feeling thought* every moment, and focus on what you want – not what you don't want.

- Joseph Campbell: "If you do follow your bliss, you put yourself on a kind of track that has been there all the while waiting for you, and the life you ought to be living is the one you are living… I say follow your bliss and don't be afraid."

# Question Section #4: Higher-Energy Assistants / Assistance

Many cultures over time have reported the existence of angels, guides, master teachers, and other evolved helpers. Much clinical data and many firsthand experiences further indicate their reality. I prefer the term *higher-energy assistants / assistance* to describe these advanced nonearthly beings / energies.

From a more religious or spiritual viewpoint, these higher beings are seen as *assistants with celestial bodies and abilities*. From a more secular perspective, this help can be viewed as *higher-energy assistance*. The term *assistance* may help those who aren't comfortable with traditional religious images of angels and other evolved beings. However you envision this help, those higher, faster, and more refined energies may provide support and guidance – especially when invited to do so.

### Articles
*#73 Angels and Higher-Energy Assistance*

*#79 Changing Worlds in Just 8 Days*

*#91 Pause and Remember*

**Books:** *Soul Proof, Greater Reality Living*

**Audio Programs:** *Ask Your Soul, G. O.D. and Angels*

***Q#1: Do angels, guides, and master teachers really exist?***

A#1: Cross-culturally, many religious / spiritual wisdom sources have taught about the reality of these highly evolved beings. In addition, good clinical evidence from multiple sources indicates they exist. After having near death experiences or Life Between Lives[R] sessions, many people report being energized, healed, and comforted. They describe this help as coming from – at least in part – angels, guides, and master teachers. Many evidential mediums describe receiving assistance from their own angels and guides and those of the person getting the reading.

Sir William Barrett, a professor of physics at the Royal College of Science in Dublin, wrote the book *Deathbed Visions*. Barrett reported that children whose bodies were dying often described angels as not having wings. He saw this as validation that they were actually having angelic visitations. If their perceptions were just based on hope or what they had been told, why wouldn't angels be described as having large white wings as depicted in art and literature?

In addition, *many firsthand experiences of angelic assistance* have been reported, some of which were *spiritually transformative*. That means the persons experiencing the angelic visits were often significantly improved in lasting ways. Such visits have been described in numerous articles, books, and documentaries.

Some people doubt the existence of angels because of ancient depictions as them being very tall and having wings. However, those well-established images may not be accurate. Perhaps people saw bright light emanating from their aura and thought it was wings.

In 2019, I conducted a series of interdimensional communication experiments in which one of the collaborators was purportedly a female angel. I can't usually sense otherworldly beings, but I relaxed and let my vision blur a bit. As I looked toward where she was supposed to be, three visual images flashed in my mind's eye in a fraction of a second: a beautiful blonde-haired woman of average height, a twelve-foot-tall woman with white wings, then a myriad of colors and energy swirling about. I later learned that three evidential mediums who had worked with this angel reported seeing the same sequence of images.

As I will discuss in Question Section #5, *how energy **appears** to manifest depends on the observer's beliefs, state of awareness and perspective / observation point.* That might explain why angels, guides, and master teachers have been sensed as winged beings, multi-colored light, or feelings of unfathomable love and regard.

However you envision this help, there is good evidence that higher, faster, and more refined energies provide support and guidance.

### Q#2: If angels really exist and help us, why don't they help more often?

A#2: In 1994, I experienced what I considered to be the grace and beauty of an angel's visit. While writing early one morning to complete my first book, I looked for a quote from *The Bible.* While searching through my books from theology school days, I couldn't find it – even in my *Concordance* of Biblical references.

Then I suddenly felt ecstatic for no apparent reason and heard a slight rustling. In my peripheral vision, I saw a white gauzy form like the fine lacework of a wedding dress. But as I turned to see it more clearly, it was gone. I felt energized and interpreted this as a sign that my work was in flow with Divine will and my highest missions.

**Immediately afterwards, I opened the Bible to the exact page needed and my eyes went directly to the verses I sought**... Hebrews

2:6-7 that asks of Creator: "What is man, that Thou art mindful of him?... Thou made him a little lower than the angels..." That seemed magical, miraculous, and like an angelic encounter to me.

Immediately afterwards, the very question that you raised began forming in my mind. *Before I could even complete the thought*, the following answers popped up:

1. Angels and other higher-energy assistants do not impose their will on you. If you make poor decisions that hurt or kill your body, that is your choice.

2. You will receive more assistance when you ask for it.

3. Realize that help may not arrive how, when, and where you expect it.

4. You will never know how often you are helped since assistance can be preventive, subtle, and undetectable.

5. You may have, before coming to earth, chosen significant challenges to assist spiritual growth. Higher-energy assistants / assistance wouldn't interfere with this plan.

6. Earth is designed to be a place of learning. Those lessons would be too easy or negated if all suffering were prevented.

## Q#3: How can I receive guidance from angels and other higher beings?

A#3. Use this four-step process and modify as you feel led:

- *How do you ask for help?* Get relaxed and centered, then express gratitude for love, support, and guidance. Rather than supplicative prayers, I prefer heartfelt requests accompanied by appreciation. Then remain receptive to assistance that – all things considered – arrives in the right way and time.

- *Who do you ask?* Some people prefer getting assistance directly from E.L.G.O.D. / the Light. Others are more comfortable with *intermediaries:* saints, angels, guides, and / or master teachers. Still others believe that *using your inner wisdom and formidable resources* is best. Since all life is one and interconnected, distinctions between you and higher-energy assistants may not be as great as you think. I cast as wide a net as possible and ask for help from all of the above.

- *How can you become more aware of assistance?* Use prayer, meditation, time in nature, and other centering practices to *quiet your brain* so you can hear wise responses from within and all around. Perceiving assistance can be as simple as: ask, give thanks, stay alert, use it wisely, and share it with others.

- *How do you use it?* Upgrade your life, serve others, make the world a better place, and enjoy this extraordinary earthly experience. Focus on the highest-energy emotions and ways of being that you can: peace, joy, love, compassion, gratitude, enthusiasm, and enlightenment.

I created the *Ask Your Soul, G. O.D. and Angels* audio program to detect guidance and assistance from your inner self, higher-energy assistants, and The Divine One. Used over time, these sessions can deepen your awareness of and interaction with them.

# Question Section #5: The Nature of Reality

What is the most absolute nature of reality? Some ancient religious and spiritual wisdom sources considered answers to this question to be *ineffable*, that is, incapable of being expressed in words. That's why they often used metaphors, parables, and other figurative descriptions. Unfortunately, those stories are sometimes confusing and subject to various interpretations. In addition, some people take these stories literally and / or use them out of context. Predictably, major differences in opinions about this question exist.

Hindu rishis, whose view of the universe predated similar quantum physics' hypotheses by several millennia, viewed life as One. The Creator and Sustainer of all life, they said, was like a cosmic artist who creates beautiful and vast paintings. When those are completed, they are set aside to make room for new canvasses. Alternately, The Infinite can be seen as a master potter who shapes clay into vessels. Some are useful while others break and are recast.

When The One inhales, these pre-A.D. spiritual explorers said, there appears to be nothingness. When It exhales, the world seems replete with a myriad of formed manifestations. A beloved spiritual teacher Ram Dass, AKA Richard Alpert PhD, said that people and all life forms are 'just patterns of energy'.

One of my favorite answers to the question about the nature of reality came from legendary jazz bass player Stanley Clarke. In his song *Life Is Just a Game*, he sings: "So life is just a game and there are many ways to play, and all you do is choose." Ultimately, life can be seen as *a master game*, a series of experiences designed to help you more deeply realize your true nature. Once you have awakened sufficiently, you can demonstrate *'The Great News'* no matter what is going on around you.

Do you choose – moment by moment and day by day – to see yourself as an integral, ever-expanding, beloved, and eternal part of Life Itself? Or do you see yourself as a helpless and hopeless victim who lives only a few years on a chaotic planet before it all ends?

**Which view you adopt shapes your personal reality and perceptions of the greater reality.**

From a systems theory perspective, what ultimately exists is energy and information that is stored ad infinitum. This info-energy is stored – to use different terms – in the zero-point field, Akashic records, space, and quantum vacuums. This information can be accessed and experienced in ways that seems as real and immediate, or even more so, than this earthly one.

From a religious viewpoint, the nature of reality is Creator, love, and light. From a quantum mechanics view, reality occurs on the cusp of rapid shifts between solid particles and formless waves. *How that appears to manifest depends on who is observing, from where, their intention, and the quality of their perceptions.*

## Articles
*#11 Expanding Your View of Life*

*#58 It's Just a Game: Optimally Handling Life's Biggest Challenges*

## The Nature of Reality

*#68 The Big Picture of Life*

*#72 Greater Reality Living*

*#100 Enlightenment*

**Books:** *Greater Reality Living, The Big Picture of Life*

**Audio Programs:** *Ask Your Soul, G. O.D., and Angels; Holistic Breathing; Past Life Regression*

**Q#1: My church teaches that we should only trust God to reveal answers about life. Why do you try to know what only God can?**

A#1: Some people who adhere to conservative religious teachings agree with you; no judgment or criticism from me. I attended a fundamentalist church for several years and understand that mindset. It seems to especially work for people who: (1) were taught as a youth that reality consists of a short time on earth followed by heaven or hell for eternity; (2) have close family and friends who believe the same way, and (3) frequently hear sermons about (1).

In this way of thinking, much — if not all — that happens in life is planned and overseen by God. If you are comfortable with those viewpoints, you may not want to read any further.

I don't try to convince anyone to change their views. Rather, I share what I have learned so people can make *more informed decisions* about what they believe. When faced with tough challenges, some of my conservatively religious patients found their beliefs didn't make sense or provide comfort. Some were motivated to learn different views about the nature of reality.

**Q#2: Why should I care about the nature of reality? If I know that life is all happening here and now, isn't that enough?**

A#2: Perhaps not. As with the person who asked the last question, there's no need to look any further if you are comfortable with your worldview. However, many people have found that **understanding more about life helps it make more sense**. Put another way, the more you learn about life, the more you realize just how safe, meaningful, and magnificent it is. And the more you realize that, the more grateful you feel.

To paraphrase William Blake: 'If the doors of perception were cleansed, everything would appear as it is, Infinite. For people have closed themselves up, till they see all things thro' narrow chinks of their cavern.' Plato's *Allegory of the Cave* used similar images: a chained prisoner in a dark cave believes that life is limited to the shadows cast by the fire behind her. After breaking free, she finds an entire new world that has always been there waiting to be discovered.

I agree that, in a very real sense, everything is happening here and now. As such, living in the present moment most of the time is an excellent strategy for optimizing your earthly experience. Knowing more about the nature of reality can help you know and do that.

*Many people don't realize* **how full and big Life Unfolding is**. The term *greater reality* includes: (1) people, animals, minerals, and plants on earth; (2) planets, moons, stars, galaxies, nebulae, and beyond; (3) energy along and beyond the electromagnetic spectrum; (4) love, memories, emotions, intentions, and other personal attributes; (5) E.L.G.O.D.; (6) all stored information and energy that, depending on the observer's perspective, may be viewed as earthly or otherworldly experiences.

## The Nature of Reality

Understanding that you are an integral part of all this is inspiring, comforting, and instructive.

**Q#3: You state, "Humans are not nearly as 'solid' as earthly sense organs report. We largely consist of subatomic particles, energy, and waves of light amidst lots of space." I thought that space was empty.**

A#3: Actually, my understanding is that 'space' is quite full. In that sense, the terms *space and vacuum* are misleading.

Gary E. Schwartz PhD uses the term *info-energy system* as a shorthand term for all the energy and information that can be stored in space. In his book *The Living Energy Universe*, he described all life as **alive, evolving, and eternal** in a dynamic system in which nothing is lost.

Professor Erwin Laszlo uses the term *Akashic or A-Field* with a nod to Hindu teachers who knew about these topics many centuries ago. I first heard the term 'The Field of All Possibilities' from Deepak Chopra MD; it remains one of my favorites for describing all that exists that may be stored in space.

David Bohm PhD was a brilliant scientist, quantum physicist, colleague of Einstein's, and author of *Wholeness and The Implicate Order*. Dr. Bohm described reality as like *a plenum soup*, a sea of energy with periodic ripples that may – depending on the observer – *appear* to be an earthly or other experience.

With my strong religious and theological background, I also appreciate more spiritual terms. **Panentheism, the view that Creator is all and in all, makes the most sense to me.** From this perspective, supposedly empty space is filled with The Light / E.L.G.O.D. that extends beyond both time and space.

**Q#4: I hear that other dimensions are not far from us. Is this so?**

A#4: That's one sense about the nature of reality that I get from several sources. Imagine that life is like a giant basketball. What we call life on earth in 2022 is one thin cross-section of that ball. Other dimensions / time-space scenarios / realms may be *just a slice away*. (Oh no, this is sounding like a pizza commercial!) Despite reports to the contrary by the limited human brain, all of life may be occurring or available in the here and now. When perceived fully and accurately, the most absolute nature of reality may be *a unified whole throughout time*.

**Q#5: If it's an illusion that the world is a mess, then why should we try to improve it? Aren't things really perfect and the way they are supposed to be?**

A#5: This is a very big and important question so please stay with me as I share my answers with the assumption that you *a 15%er*. Saying 'it's an illusion that the world is a mess' is an overly logical / simplified way of putting it. Many people suffer in ways that are very real and painful to them. Telling them that things are perfect may elicit resentment and anger.

I'll frame my answers from: (1) a limited earthly perspective, and (2) a *unitive consciousness* view.

    1. *A limited earthly perspective* makes it seem that our world is a hopeless and tragic mess. Over time, this misinformed view can engender lower-energy emotions and ways of being. Actions are taken from an 'us versus them' mentality, for example, the war on poverty, the war on drugs, the war against disease, etc. Actions motivated by fear, anger, and hopelessness can't optimally address problems. Uninformed views may not take into account that:

a. life continues after bodily death

b. all life is one and is sacredly interconnected

c. suffering is a great way to learn and grow

d. seeming victims may have volunteered for the growth and service opportunities

e. only part of a person's life force is involved in difficult scenarios

f. apparent earthly events are actually energy / light / information manifesting in a variety of ways depending on who is having the experience

2. *A unitive consciousness view* is enjoyed by more evolved persons with an expanded comprehension of the greater reality. They see, at least some of the time, beyond the illusion that the world is a mess. Partially remembering (a) – (f) above as often as possible makes a huge difference. Recalling the big picture of life amidst difficulties allows them to help others and focus on the highest feeling thoughts, words, and actions.

An old Hindu saying states, 'There is nothing to do, and nothing is left undone.' A Taoist version of this is, 'When nothing is done, nothing is left undone.' At first glance, these sayings can seem like gibberish. I assume that alterations in the original meanings crept in when translating into English. My sense is that wise ones behind these sayings recognized the factors discussed in the two prior paragraphs.

Seeming dilemmas occur when conclusions made by 'the head' / brain differ from those by the inner heart / soul. Ram Dass described the plight of awakening when someone suffers. The head objectively says: 'Karma' while the heart says 'I am so sorry. How can I help?'

If pressed for a definitive answer, I would say that – all things considered from the most absolute view of reality – life *is* unfolding perfectly. That answer can sound horribly ignorant and cruel to a person whose *loved one's body* was murdered or died by suicide. (The loved one continues living in another realm, remember?) I hope this paints a sufficiently broad picture so you can address this seeming paradox: life is unfolding perfectly AND, at the same time, all hands-on deck are needed to address the suffering and injustices.

**Q#6: Do we create our own realities? If so, do we come to earth to have "real" experiences, not just the mind-imagined ones on the Other Side?**

A#6: I would say *you **co-create** your reality* since some aspects of your life may already be in motion. For example, choosing to visit earth requires that birth, death, and at least some suffering is *built into the package*. However, you likely can co-create the quality and quantity of your earthly visit.

**Before coming to earth**, influences are exerted via: (1) pre-birth planning; (2) past experiences; and (3) your level of consciousness. **After arriving**, additional co-creative factors include: (1) how well you listen to your inner guidance and that of higher-energy assistants and Source; (2) daily choices about how you think, speak, and act; (3) taking responsibility for your life; (4) how quickly and well you learn from 'mistakes'.

In general, the degree to which you understand *'The Great News'* and live accordingly determines whether you seem to be paddling up or down stream during your earthly experience.

As indicated by your quotation marks, the word 'real' is a tricky one, isn't it? This supposedly real / solid earthly experience is just as illusory as those in more *just mind-imagined* / etheric realms. My current thinking is that *all experiences, whether they seem to be formed or formless, are mind-imagined.* They may best be considered as **virtual reality experiences** that timeless energy / souls choose for purposes of service, adventure, growth, and enjoyment.

However, the illusion of solidity, separateness, and death can be very convincing during an earthly visit. Those seem so 'real' that many may reject this discussion as nonsensical. That can create a dense, uninformed, and fearful mass consciousness with resultant effects on people.

*Earthly experiences may have a greater intensity and sense of physicality* versus those on other planes of consciousness. My guess is that whether sensations seem more 'real' or 'mind-imagined' depends on the experiencer's level of awareness. Those with advanced energies might enjoy chocolate, lovemaking, and sunsets in other dimensions just as much as on earth.

Whether an experience seems formed / physical / solid OR formless / spiritual / ethereal is ultimately *in the eye of the beholder.* A limited nervous system in an imbalanced body / brain will usually only perceive lower and slower energies that appear solid. But there is so much more to life than that.

Regarding the "realness" of an earthly experience, Ram Dass said: 'You know how a dream can seem so real until you wake up? Well, just wait until you wake up from this one.'

**Q#7: The terms 'beginner' and 'advanced' souls imply they are of various ages. Haven't all souls existed forever since there is only ONE Soul and no time in eternity?**

A#7: The terms 'beginner, intermediate, and advanced' refer to *how evolved* a person / soul is – not how long she / he / it existed. That's why I avoid the potentially confusing terms 'young soul' and 'old soul'. In terms of time of existence, a 'newer soul' may evolve quickly while an 'older soul' might repeat the same mistakes and thus not advance as much over the same period of time.

(Note: Please recall the **Levels of Energy / Soul Development** glossary definition. The terms beginner, intermediate, and advanced are not judgmental, nor do they imply a hierarchy of better or worse. They are descriptions of where a person / soul currently is for knowing and showing who they are and why they are here. Everyone is an important and sacred part of the One. However, not all people realize and demonstrate this equally. These are not fixed levels but, rather, can change as soon as a person understands more about the greater reality and lives accordingly.)

What is your definition of the term 'ONE Soul'? I'm not being critical or disrespectful, but there is a need for more accurate statements about the nature of reality. If you are referring to One Mind / Source, then I agree about its unitive nature. However, E.L.G.O.D. can spin off new aspects continually. Watch videos from Hubble showing gigantic nebulae – called *star nurseries* – that spew out gases and particles with the potential for forming new stars. I envision this as how new souls are continually formed or, perhaps, reformed over time.

I've seen statements that *'all souls have existed forever'*, but is that really true? Perhaps a better statement based on known scientific facts is that *energy cannot be destroyed but it can change outward form.* When did a snippet of energy / life force take form as a supposedly separate 'soul'? And is that an ongoing process or were all souls created at once?

Can that energy shift from one soul / person to another? Might souls / people eventually choose to merge into the One / the Collective Consciousness, and end the wheel of cyclical life experiences? Or might their consciousness become so evolved that they naturally morph into higher modes of expression that don't involve physical-appearing incarnations? I've not found any consensus to answers about such questions.

Regarding your words about 'no time in eternity', I would put it this way:

1. Time is only relatively real, but it is useful for functioning on this *time-altered planet.*

2. Time on earth may be different from time in afterlife realms.

Physicists and astronomers speak of 'spacetime events'. Dr. Gary Schwartz notes common NDE reports of hearing music during visits to the Light. He points out that *music requires timing for proper spacing and orchestration.* As such, the 'no time' statement may be another one that needs further investigation.

Ultimately, we can't fully fathom these things from our limited earthly perspectives. It's like asking when and how did life come into being. It's fun to consider such matters. But, at the end of the day, it's important to focus on basics. My list includes remembering who I am, loving myself and others, learning, growing, sharing my greatest gifts, and enjoying life.

Put another way: *Before enlightenment, chop wood and carry water. After enlightenment, chop wood and carry water.*

**Q#8: Some people say that, after the physical body dies, we merge with Source and no longer retain our individuality. Wouldn't that destroy any hope of seeing my deceased fiancé again? Also, if that view is true, who are mediums talking to when they connect with the 'departed'?**

A#8: Regarding *merged versus separate individual,* perhaps it doesn't have to be either / or. Michael Newton PhD did a great job of describing how one's awareness / energy may manifest in different times and place while – simultaneously – never leaving the One. About 65,000 Life Between Lives⁽ᴿ⁾ sessions have been conducted with clients from 48 countries by therapists using a total of 21 different languages. Impressively, these clients describe 'spiritual' realms with a remarkable consistency. Such a high degree of *inter-rater reliability* among so many diverse clients makes this data even more credible.

Based on this data, Newton stated that only about 20% of a person's total energy is usually involved in an earthly experience. The rest may enjoy other parts of The Field of All Possibilities as a plant, animal, formed or formless being, or *undifferentiated potential*. **It is the latter that may most seem like merging with All That Is.**

Clinical studies and postmaterial communication technology findings indicate that PMPs retain their memory, individuality, preferences, sense of humor, love, information, **and much more.** They also have – *or can have, depending on their intentions and interactions* – physicality, mass, and density. This is what mediums can sense and how PMPs can relay specific information to those who receive the reading.

As you say, *if individuality is completely lost, what hope is there for reunions with loved ones after bodily death?* According to Ken Ring PhD, there have been approximately ten thousand documented near death experiencers. And many of these documented NDE reports describe having reunions with loved ones. What kind of Creator wouldn't provide choices to continue loving relationships?

(Documented NDEr means that, while clinically dead and with their eyes closed, patients correctly perceived events that happened in or around the hospital. This is especially impressive when occurring – as it has many times – with little children and blind people.

Researchers ensured that these NDErs could not have accurately sensed these events unless, indeed, consciousness exists independently of normal brain functioning. To learn more, see *Lessons from the Light* by Ken Ring PhD.)

*You and everyone else are integral parts of Source Energy right now and always.* The more you deeply know that, the less important concerns and questions about details become. You can trust that – however life plays out through eternity – it surely will be fair, safe, meaningful, and magnificent. Creator's design is all that and much more.

**Q#9: I have read that advanced souls don't have to stay on this earthly plane very long. Do you agree with this statement?**

A#9: Thank you for thinking I'm wise enough to know the answer to such a deep question. However, that is the emerging picture from multiple sources of clinical data. The title of my Q & A for the *Helping Parents Heal* newsletter is: *Evolved Souls Don't Need Long Earthly Lives*. This title reflects the possibility that children who pass on may be advanced beings. At the least, they might have been on a mission to help many people. Many bereaved parents have independently described corroborating signs, for example, that their children:

1. had a different look in their eyes, as though they were very wise despite their youth

2. were more compassionate, thoughtful, and loving than most children

3. had a sense of urgency to do and experience as much as possible – as though they knew their time on earth was limited

4. drew artwork depicting them going up into the sky to join waiting angels

5. made statements such as 'I will only be here for a short while'

It makes sense that more advanced persons would *need* fewer earthly classes. They might not require staying very long or coming to earth at all. Evolved ones may *volunteer* to visit earth to assist growth and learning of beginner souls. More advanced people may already know – at least in their unconscious and / or super-conscious minds – that they are deathless, integral parts of Source Energy, and interconnected with all life. Knowing this and the other great news accompanying a greater reality perspective makes their earthly visit quite different from the 'average' person.

Out of love, more evolved souls / persons may manifest part of their energy in a virtual reality-like visit to earth. They know their bodies will likely suffer, but also know that's a small price to pay for potentially helping many people and our planet. For example, *bodhisattvas* are considered in Buddhism to be highly evolved ones who are well along the path of becoming fully realized. They didn't have to come to earth for karmic reasons. Rather, they chose to serve and teach here to relieve suffering and assist the greatest good of all sentient beings.

# Question Section #6: 'Heaven' and 'Hell'

A synthesis of ancient and contemporary information allows us to understand what 'heaven' and 'hell' really are. Over two thousand years ago, Aramaic and Hebrew meanings of those words meant, in part, *how you feel – now and in the afterlife – depending on your predominant thoughts, words, and deeds*. If you are **mostly** good and loving – no one is perfect – you will feel more heavenly: happy, peaceful, grateful, etc. If you are angry, fearful, and bitter much of the time, your life will seem more hellish. These states of mind were not considered to be just physical places, one way up in the sky, the other at the earth's core.

In the 21st century, many documented near death experiencers describe a key part of their time in the Light. **During a life review, they see and feel** all the good or bad they created while on earth. This experience can be heavenly or hellish depending on how they lived. After recovering from clinical death, many NDErs return with a strong knowing they have been given a sacred opportunity to do better. They want to improve their lives for many reasons. When their bodies irreversibly die, their life reviews will reflect that improvement.

I hope my answers below help you increasingly enjoy and spread heavenly ways of being.

## Articles
*#14 Heaven and Hell... What Are They Really?*

*#42 What Is the Afterlife for Evil Doers Like?*

*#46 Unforgivable Sin?*

*#65 Karma*

*#67 Contrast Souls*

**Books:** *Soul Proof, Greater Reality Living, The Big Picture of Life, The Eleven Questions*

**Audio Programs:** *Life Review Technique; Ask Your Soul, G.O.D., and Angels*

***Q#1: I could never believe that a loving God would allow even one person to suffer in hell forever. But some churches still teach this?!***

A#1: Like you, many people are horrified by the image of a God who would allow anyone to experience eternal torment. They feel that a caring Creator wouldn't work that way, but are concerned by religious teachings to the contrary. Refuting fear-based teachings can be especially difficult when taught such bizarre notions as a child. Some denominations still teach that a fiery eternal hell, or cessation of consciousness, exists for those who don't believe and / or live a certain way. They are in the minority but are very vociferous so their hellish messages impact a lot of people.

Most Christian denominations consider **hell to be a metaphor for how we feel when separated from Source**. Most of us have experienced the personal darkness that accompanies not living congruently with our highest natures. However, as the prodigal son story in *The Bible* teaches, we are instantly met with open arms whenever we return Home / remember who we are. The Light's plan of *wholeness for all* is not thwarted by time or space. Even if there were a fiery eternal hell, how could those in 'heaven' enjoy eternity while knowing that many are suffering endless torment?

Does this sound like the best a loving and wise Creator and Sustainer of All Life can do?

You can now safely discard erroneous teachings that blaspheme G.O.D. and scare people away from wanting a personal relationship with their Source. My reassurance is based on the majority of religions and denominations, reports from near death experiencers, evidential medium sessions, after death communications, Life Between Lives sessions, and common sense about how a celestial parent would operate.

### Q#2: If heaven is so perfect, why would we ever want to come to earth?

A#2: Ding, ding, ding! That's the million-dollar question that my ten-year-old daughter asked many years ago. The short answer is to keep evolving and help others. There are a few sides to the longer answer. Heaven is not a place with a separate zip code and location. It is, first and foremost, *a state of consciousness*, a higher realization that you are one with All That Is right now and forevermore. **When you really get that, you can experience a heavenly life anytime and anywhere.**

Granted, It may be easier to know and show that great news while living in non-earthly realms. Why? Because the human brain is so limited in perceiving the full nature of reality. Suffering is ensured if we solely trust the brain's reports about life. Remembering the big picture of life can be much easier in spiritual realms where it's more obvious that you are also loved, assisted, and guided by soulmates, angels, guides, and the Light.

As you know, earthly experiences can **seem** so chaotic and cruel. Even so, there are **numerous good reasons why people choose to come to earth,** for example:

1. Learn that *much suffering is caused by misinformed beliefs based on your brain's limited perceptions.* Fear, hopelessness, excessive grief, and other lower-energy emotions are **just feelings** based on misunderstandings about the nature of life.

2. To better *appreciate and freely choose* love, peace, and vitality after firsthand experiences of hate, turmoil, and depression.

3. To practice 'walking the talk'. It's one thing to remember it's all good / G.O.D. when you can see more of the greater reality AND others around you can as well. *The real test comes when you and many people around you suffer with spiritual amnesia.* An earthly experience allows you to see how deeply you really know the most important lessons in life. You can test your degree of enlightenment and see what happens when 'the rubber hits the road.'

4. To assist the evolution of One Mind. *Creator isn't a completed product.* Rather, She is an ever-expanding phenomenon. Insights and growth from your struggles may get reported back to Source and others. Is that worth a brief and relatively illusory visit to earth?

My statements about good reasons for coming to earth may initially sound too abstract or naive to you. If so, I hope they make more sense after fully reading this book and using the experiential audio programs. I know that some people suffer from starvation, disease, abuse, and murder. However, it has been demonstrated – by Drs. Victor Frankl and Edith Eva Eger in Nazi concentration camps, for example – that *even this* can be overcome with an evolved heart and mind. Remember, too, that those suffering may have volunteered to experience that for karmic, growth, and service reasons.

**Q#3: You say that everyone who dies goes to heaven, but what happens to those who aren't fit for heaven yet? Surely pedophiles and murderers don't get a free pass and go to heaven? If that happened, heaven wouldn't be perfect.**

A#3: If, indeed, I said or wrote that 'everyone who dies goes to heaven', please show me where so I can edit it. Many years ago, I didn't know as much about the afterlife and my terms were sometimes imprecise.

'Heaven' is primarily a state of mind, a level of awareness that shapes how you live and treat others. A heavenly state of being can be experienced no matter where you are living and what is going on around you.

Everyone has an afterlife. That may feel heavenly or hellish depending on one's consciousness at the time of bodily death. Pedophiles and murderers would, starting with their life reviews, **see and feel** the harm they caused to others. Depending on a number of factors, they may languish in torment for a very long time. In this way, there are temporary and self-induced hells.

However, those who commit horrible acts toward others may have been molested or abused themselves. Biochemical imbalances, impetuous pre-birth selections of body / brain, and other causes may increase the probabilities of a sweet child becoming a criminal abuser.

**Knowledgeable and compassionate people on earth understand this. Surely Creator does as well.**

From a limited earthly vantage point, you and I can't see all the factors and agendas involved. We can't know who is 'fit for heaven' and don't have to be concerned about justice being meted out fairly. We each have a full-time job living in loving and balanced ways. That is why various spiritual wisdom sources teach: 'Why do you focus on the speck of wood in your neighbor's eye instead of the log in your own?'

The more expansive your view of life, the more you'll realize that *everyone is doing the best they think they can given their level of consciousness and resources at the time.* This helps explain why some people who endure severe challenges rise above them while others do not.

The notion of 'heaven as perfect' reflects archaic teachings that were designed to control people. After all, who wouldn't want to experience a perfect place forever versus eternal suffering? It would be worth putting your money in the offering plate, and muting your inner voice, right? However, notions of 'heaven' as perfect are overly simplistic. For example, some consider that to be walking on golden streets and endlessly praising 'God' while people of other religions burn for eternity. How could a truly loving person enjoy such a place?

Whether living on earth or elsewhere, some people enjoy a wonderful and heavenly life. Others experience a hellish existence as they face what they have done to others and learn difficult lessons. *Heaven and hell, then, are not the result of **where** we live but **how** we live.*

**Q#4: In my church, we are taught that God is loving and forgiving, but we may not go straight to heaven. We might go to purgatory. Doesn't this conflict with the teachings of Jesus?**

A#4: I agree that Source is loving, but it's even better than that. The Divine doesn't need to forgive us because She never judges or condemns us in the first place. But we do need to forgive ourselves and others.

Purgatory may best be seen as *a waiting period* after passing on. Teaching about that may be your church's acknowledgement of different possibilities for what happens after bodily death. Some recently 'deceased' persons may need a longer *sorting out process* before moving away from earth. Others may want to stay closer to grieving loved ones so they can attempt to comfort them. For various reasons, some who just dropped their earthly form may not choose to enter The Light immediately. The concept of purgatory covers these and other possible scenarios that might sound like being stuck between worlds in a sort of netherworld.

However, teachings about purgatory may also be a way for churches to raise more money. I'm not saying that is the case for your church. However, as a teen, I watched my relatives – who really couldn't afford it – fill offering plates during my grandpa's funeral. Why? So the priest would pray my grandpa who – in his later years mainly attended 'The Church of Jack Daniels' – into heaven.

Regarding conflicts with the concept of purgatory and the teachings of Jesus, *The Bible* has been greatly changed over the millennia through translations, interpretations, and outright changes. I attended theology school and took every Biblical history class offered. After 1 1/2 years, the lead professor summarized: 'As you now know, there is very little we factually know about what Jesus did or did not say.' (Why didn't they tell me that on the first day? I could have saved a lot of time and money.)

I have a strong sense, and have since a child, about what a spiritual master like Jesus would really teach. Likewise, many elders have shared with me *what they knew in their heart* that a master teacher would say. Here's the short list…

1. Love one another and yourself.

2. Serve Creator by helping others and caring for animals and nature.

3. Follow the Golden Rule.

4. Remember that you are one with Source and sacredly interconnected with all life.

5. Release fear and remember that death is not an end.

6. Share your greatest gifts and let your light shine to brighten the world.

When you know this list and live accordingly, you are free and filled with the peace that passes all understanding. Your brief time on earth will be experienced as from a foundation of granite, not shifting sand.

**Q#5: I am reading a book about what happens after we die. One of the chapters involves NDE's that take place in hell: screaming, agony, and total blackness. Two of the people in hell asked God to free them and they saw the Light. Why wouldn't everyone do the same thing? I've had one long panic attack after reading that. Several loved ones passed on in the last year and I'm terrified about what they are experiencing.**

A#5: How sad that you and others must fear for loved ones who pass on. Religion, clinicians, and science need to do a better job of teaching about the greater reality. I hope the information in this book helps you to release instead of embrace fear.

Reports of hellish NDEs are rare and may be the result of several factors. Some researchers in this field – Raymond Moody MD,

PhD and Eben Alexander MD, for example – consider that these reports are largely due to *a carry-over of beliefs that people had while on earth*. If they strongly believed in a fiery eternal abode and feared they might end up there, that might be **their initial perception / experience after dying**. If they had stayed clinically dead longer, they may have seen that The Light is loving and accepting, not vengeful and judgmental.

The quality of the afterlife is determined by one's degree of consciousness at the time of transitioning from earth. When the body of a serial murderer dies, he may experience what seems like eternal torment based on his self-judgment. This sets up a hellish life review as the abuser sees *and feels* the pain he caused others. That may be lessened by a number of factors such as mitigating circumstances, true repentance, and making amends. It can take time for people to forgive themselves. Until they do, they may judge themselves as guilty and deserving of punishment. That might seem like a very long hell but it's self-inflicted and temporary.

To be clear, E.L.G.O.D. and higher-energy assistants don't require everlasting punishment for those who commit heinous crimes. More evolved material persons understand that a child who became imbalanced due to mental illness or abuse could become an abuser. They know that prescription drug reactions or severe emotional trauma can cause a person to hurt others.

If some people understand that, surely the Creator and Sustainer of All Life does. That's why G.O.D., angels, and other higher beings stand ready to love, comfort, and assist healing whenever the person is ready and asks for help. **There are no locks on the doors to 'hell' except for locks in the minds of those who believe they are worthless sinners who deserve severe punishment.** Unfortunately, some religious denominations reinforce that belief.

Why wouldn't everyone ask to enter the Light? For the same reasons that everyone doesn't ask for Divine assistance during their earthly experiences: fear, misinformation, lack of awareness, and self-judgment. Ignorant and fear-based religious teachings have perpetuated those factors instead of sharing how wonderfully life is set up. People may not know about the welcoming Light and wonderful open-ended opportunities after bodily death. Others may feel they deserve to burn and suffer for a while or forever.

Whatever the case, as soon as anyone asks for help, The Light is always there to welcome them Home. Search for 'Rev. Howard Storm's NDE' to read and watch his personal story. I was blessed to hear him speak twice in person. His testimonial is a perfect example of how unconditionally loving and caring The Divine / Life is.

**Q#6: This question is about "nones", those people who are not affiliated with any particular religion. This usually happens because they understandably perceive organized religion as defective in many ways. Can these people have positive afterlife experiences?**

A#6: Religious affiliation, or the lack thereof, isn't a crucial factor in the quality of afterlife experiences. **What matters most is the level of consciousness and predominant thoughts, words, and actions.** Near death experiencers – whether they are believers, agnostics, or atheists – are just as likely to have blissful encounters with The Light. The movie *What Dreams May Come* does a great job of showing, despite degrees of belief or disbelief, how the afterlife may manifest. It especially addresses that 'hell' is primarily a state of mind that can be upgraded via love and other higher intentions.

# Question Section #7:
# 'The Devil' and 'Evil Spirits'

Fear about a powerful 'devil' who tricks and negatively influences us at every turn is another common theme in questions I've received. After all, how can we really trust a 'God' who created a super powerful evil being who wreaks havoc on His children? As is often the case, distorted 'religious' teachings from the Dark Ages and even B.C. are the culprit. As a youth, I remember listening to *Biblical* stories about an evil formidable opponent to Creator and thinking how bizarre that sounded.

Fortunately, a wealth of clinical research and firsthand experiences refute the notion that any such evil being exists. Most religions and denominations, and their underlying theological and philosophical views, agree. The problem is that fear-based denominations, although a distinct minority, are very good at scaring people. Why would they do that? One reason is so more people join 'the one true way' church and donate money to 'save their souls'.

In the past, some powerful religious influencers viewed people as inherently sinful, ignorant, and in need of protection from 'the devil'. They tried the 'fear of burning with satan forever' approach to control people. How is that working so far? A better way is to help people remember who they are, why they are here, and Who walks beside them always. There's no place in this formula for a giant red-skinned and horned boogeyman with a pitchfork.

I use single quotation marks and lower-case letters for 'devil' for reasons described above. **Instead of 'evil spirit', I prefer the term 'imbalanced entity'.** There are immature, mentally ill, and imbalanced humans on earth, right? The same appears to be true of beings in other planes of existence. I use the word 'entity' instead of PMP since these imbalanced beings may come from other places than earth. 'Imbalanced entities' are disconnected from Life and thus confused / ignorant about their nature. They are not to be feared but, rather, are in need of our compassion and prayers.

## Articles
#47 'evil spirits' and 'the devil'

**Books:** *Soul Proof, The Big Picture of Life*

**Audio Programs:** *Ask Your Soul, G. O.D., and Angels*

### Q#1: What, in your opinion, are evil spirits and the devil?

A#1: Reports from firsthand experiences claim that imbalanced entities can hurt and negatively influence people on earth. Some people believe they have been physically and / or emotionally harmed by these imbalanced entities. I don't judge their reports or minimize the stresses they felt. However, many of the cases I've heard of involve people who were intoxicated, very fearful of evil, addicted, mentally ill, obsessed with the topic, and / or involved in satanic rituals. **These factors may, *consciously or unconsciously, invite imbalanced entities in.***

Original Aramaic meanings for the words 'evil' and 'devil' were the same: *wild, chaotic, and imbalanced energy*. During the Dark Ages, 'the devil' morphed into a formidable being opposed to Creator. The term 'the devil' is still used by fundamentalist denominations and cults to describe a supposed embodiment of evil that is nearly as powerful as The Ground of All Being.

A literal 'devil' was never seriously considered by mainstream theologians, the majority of religious denominations, and most religions. While it may be convenient to blame your or the world's problems on a scary and diabolical being, contemporary evidence does not support its existence. *Is it just a coincidence that 'evil' and 'devil' are 'live' and 'lived' spelled backwards?*

**Q#2: I've read a lot about the devil and evil spirits and the need to watch out for them. What are your thoughts on this?**

A#2: Fear-based teachings about these subjects – that the original founders and integrous developers of religions would never recognize – have traumatized many people. My advice? Don't read about and dwell upon this topic. Instead, focus on good, love, and light. Every moment, *choose higher energies, emotions, and ways of being*: peace, joy, hope, gratitude, compassion, enthusiasm, and enlightenment. Those who focus on this and their oneness with Source have nothing to fear from evil-acting beings who are imbalanced unevolved, and relatively weak.

I highly recommend the movie *Oh God* for its inspirational story and theological wisdom. (How unfortunate that this movie contained more enlightened teachings than some churches.) For example, regarding beliefs about a very powerful red devil – but not a loving and powerful Creator – God, played by George Burns, said:

> Why is It so hard for you to believe? Is my physical existence anymore improbable than your own? What about all that hoo-ha with the devil a while ago from that movie? (*The Exorcist*) Nobody had any problem believing that the devil took over and existed in a little girl. All she had to do

was wet the rug, throw up some pea soup, and everybody believed. The devil you could believe, but not God? I work in my own way. I don't get inside little children; they got enough to do just being themselves.

I am heartened to see more people develop beliefs and worldviews based on love and clarity instead of fear and confusion. We all have enough to do on earth without adding a bogus horned devil into the mix.

### Q#3: My church teaches that the devil is a metaphor for evil in the world. Do you agree?

A#3: That's a better understanding than those held by conservative or fundamentalist denominations. Alternative thoughts are that 'the devil' is:

1. real and can directly influence and / or possess people.

2. a metaphor for the evil humans are capable of.

3. an archaic concept that can be twisted to justify demonizing other people.

I agree with #2 and 3. However, given the fear and history behind this concept, I recommend only using the word 'the devil' with single quotation marks and lower-case letters. This usage will remind you and others about the points made above regarding this mistaken concept.

# Question Section #8: 'Ghosts' / Interim Postmaterial Persons

*Interim Postmaterial Person (Interim PMP)* is my recommended term for 'ghost.' I know, it's different and a bit cumbersome, but much more accurate. Newer terms based on contemporary understandings can help you release archaic and erroneous notions. **Interim PMP refers to people whose bodies have died, but haven't yet moved into the Light.** After bodily death, their energy / focus may be more on earth, or between earth and the next phase of life.

The existence of interim PMPs is supported by some clinical data and evidence from firsthand experiences. In the video documentary *Sightings: The Ghost Report*, paranormal researcher Tony Cornell of Cambridge University stated: "There's a lot of fraud in this, a lot of imagination, a lot of wishful thinking. But when you strip that all out, there's about 20% hard core stuff that's exceedingly difficult to explain."

**Articles**
#104 *"Ghosts" / Interim Postmaterial Persons*

**Books:** *Soul Proof*

**Audio Program:** *Ask Your Soul, G. O.D., and Angels*

## Q#1: What are ghosts and how do they get that way?

A#1: One theory is that some people don't enter The Light after their bodies die for reasons listed below. Another view is that 'ghosts' are *echoes or reflections of negative energies* that can be associated with a house, piece of furniture, or other physical object. Since people – whether living on earth or elsewhere – are fundamentally manifestations of energy, these seemingly differing views may be largely a matter of semantics.

*The next phase of life* is one synonym for the afterlife. In the case of interim PMPs, **living between worlds may be just what they need for a while**. In old and fearful ways of thinking, the plight of 'ghosts' may have seemed like a bad thing. But is that always or ever the case?

Interim PMPs may temporarily exist on, or between earth and afterlife realms where most people go, for several reasons:

*1. During their earthly experience, they had little or no belief in the afterlife.* For example, bizarre religious teachings may have caused them to reject any notion of a Higher Power or life after death. For those who believed there is no afterlife, that can be their initial experience. Eventually, they are very likely to notice they are still conscious and, like Descartes, conclude: "I think, therefore I am."

*2. A violent or sudden death occurred,* and they were in shock when they passed on. As a result, they may not have seen The Light. Or perhaps they decided to not enter it because of fear or other reasons. The stronger one's spiritual foundation while on earth, the more likely they are prepared for such occurrences. Gandhi, for example, knew who he was and where he was going as he lay dying from gunshot wounds and repeated a word for The Divine.

3. *Concern about earthly loved ones* is another motivation for not entering the Light. The PMP may want to watch over those 'left behind' and send comfort and messages. Those with higher energies may be able to operate with love, peace, and joy whether living on earth, in the Light, or in between. So, they choose to stick around earth for a while. However, those with less evolved energies may be afraid or anxious during this netherworld time. Their lower energies can be perceived by sensitive individuals as fearful and cold.

4. *Fear about the quality of their afterlife experience* may cause recently 'departed' persons to pause before moving away from the earth plane. Those who seriously consider the possibility of an eternal place of punishment may hesitate to enter the next phase of life. The 'betwixt and between' state as an interim PMP may provide time for releasing fear-based beliefs and preparing oneself for higher realms.

5. *Needing time to ponder* may be another reason why recently 'deceased' persons delay entering the Light. They may want to chill out and process, especially after just leaving a chaotic or anxious setting.

6. *Strong negative emotions* such as jealousy, guilt, or anger existed at the time of passing on. Interim PMPs may not have wanted to enter The Light because their focus was on revenge, hatred, and other negative emotions.

7. *Addictions to **excessive** materialism, sex, alcohol, drugs, sports, etc. existed at the time of bodily death.* Recently deceased persons feared they couldn't get 'their fix' in the afterlife so they avoided moving on.

For these reasons and more, recently 'deceased' people may not be ready to move into the next phase of life. However, they can change their minds whenever they are ready.

***Q#2: My son passed on after an accidental overdose. Some books and videos about ghosts say addicts can become stuck in realms of lower vibrations / darkness and don't enter the Light. I believe he lives on, but WHERE is my concern.***

A#2: I am happy to see that you are searching for sensible answers. There are a variety of opinions about what happens to interim PMPs so it can be scary and confusing.

One reason for the spectrum of views about interim PMPs is that there isn't a 'one size fits all' answer. Consider the diversity of people on earth; the same is likely true for postmaterial persons. Before transitioning from this earthly experience, was he knowledgeable about and grounded in spiritual beliefs, or not? Was he peaceful, loving, and balanced, or not so much? Is he regularly getting blessings and prayers from loved ones on earth with encouragement to enter the Light? Or are his family and friends frozen with fear about him being alone?

It's a common belief that 'getting stuck' after passing on is a bad thing. But is it really? As reasons #3 – 5 under A#1 above indicate, there may be good reasons for taking one's time before turning the next page in life's never-ending story. After death of the body, many people recognize The Light and happily embrace it, but that path may not always be chosen. The bottom line? People can enter The Light whenever they are ready and are not penalized for waiting.

Your son is firmly embedded in eternity. He is loved and highly regarded more than you can imagine. *He is a forever being* who hit a speed bump in the road of life as many people do. (Please remember that the speed bump may have pre-planned for the growth and service opportunities therein.) He can learn from it, and hopefully others will benefit from his challenges. Please don't worry about him; instead, keep those prayers going and see him entering The Light. Contact prayer groups such as the worldwide Unity Prayer Circle and ask them to do the same.

## Q#3: Where are the angels and guides of ghosts? Why don't they help?

A#3: The Light and higher-energy assistants – angels, guides, master teachers, soulmates – are always there to assist and guide whenever asked. They may nudge, but do not force interim PMPs to move into the next phase of life. Free will is a precious part of life and those evolved helpers wouldn't deny that. That may seem uncaring until you remember that all lessons, even sad and difficult ones, can result in greater growth and wisdom. In addition, only part of a person's energy is between realms. Any time 'stuck' between realms is a relatively illusory and brief experience. So pausing before embracing The Light may not be as dire or sad as it seems.

# Question Section #9: Enlightened Religious / Spiritual Teachings

Many thousands of religions and denominations exist with an estimated 40,000 or more in Christianity alone. An unknown number of spiritual wisdom sources and centers also exist. One way to categorize them is *whether they are primarily fear or love based*. Fear-based ones preach about a judgmental 'God' who will send unbelievers and sinners to a fiery abode forever. They may also teach about love and service to others, but the fearful and judgmental parts can drown that out. Love-based religious / spiritual approaches highlight loving your neighbor and self, sharing your greatest gifts, living with peace and joy, and knowing you are one with Source.

I've attended churches in both categories and saw a world of difference between them. In my answers, I'll share what I've found to be optimal teachings that align with a Creator of unfathomable love, wisdom, power, and creativity.

## Articles
*#16 Sensible and Evidence Based Spiritual Teachings*

*#83 Am I a Christian?*

ENLIGHTENED RELIGIOUS / SPIRITUAL TEACHINGS

**Books:** *Soul Proof, Greater Reality Living*

**Audio Programs:** *Ask Your Soul, G. O.D., and Angels*

**Q#1: *How do I know which are the best spiritual teachings?***

A#1: Which ones resonate most with you? Thomas Jefferson said that wisdom is embedded in *The Bible* like diamonds in a dunghill. Other sacred texts I've seen are likewise too long and unclear. The good news is that *common threads of wisdom* exist throughout different religious and spiritual approaches. Those were termed 'the perennial philosophy' by Aldous Huxley and include:

1. know that your life does not end after physical death

2. remember you are one with E.L.G.O.D. right now

3. live accordingly:
   a.) love and take care of yourself

   b.) love, appreciate, respect, and help your neighbors

   c.) follow the Golden Rule

   d.) forgive others and yourself

   e.) know that life doesn't end after your body dies

   f.) share your special gifts and let your inner light shine

   g.) enjoy the beauty and fullness of life in the here and now

That overview rejects claims by religious denominations that you:

- are distant from Creator and could be forever separated from Her

- were born into sin because the first people sinned

- are a lowly sinner who is prone to error and poor judgment

- could suffer in eternal torment if you don't believe and / or act 'the right way'

- must accept someone else's 'one true way' to enlightenment

How can you find the best religious / spiritual center for you? Start with one that focuses on these areas and the spirit of the song *We Are One in the Spirit*: 'We are one in the Spirit, we are one in the Lord. We are one with the Spirit, we are one in the Lord. And we pray that our unity will someday be restored. And they'll know we are God's children by our love, by our love. Yes they'll know we are God's children by our love.'

(The 'pray that our unity will someday be restored' part refers to peace on earth. Wholeness / unity / oneness is how the greater reality is set up. Remembering and demonstrating that is a key for establishing unity on earth.)

**Q#2: Some religions say that suffering can help us grow spiritually. The sudden death by cancer of the only woman who has ever loved me has not caused me to grow spiritually. It has destroyed me. I have paid for therapist after therapist and got nowhere. Doctors only give anti-depressants which don't really do a lot.**

A#2: *Suffering is not a requirement unless you make it one.* Suffering *can* help you awaken, especially when you have a group of kindred spirits to assist that journey. You didn't mention how long it's been, but it can take a while to recover after the bodily death of a loved one.

You are 'in a hole' right now but can climb out of it, especially with love and support from others. This big challenge may be the primary reason why you are on earth at this time. See A#5 below for a list of religious / spiritual centers that have been helpful for me. Read articles #11, 68, 74, 75, and 77 and take action steps.

I'm not dispensing health care advice from afar for your depression, but some people have benefited from the following regimens:

    1. *Holistic Breathing Technique* to release pain and regain stuck energy (article #70)

    2. *Nutrition-Based Healing*: Thinking and grieving so much for so long can cause deficiencies of nutrients needed for optimal brain function. (article #32)

    3. *Natural Health Care*: You need a holistic team to help you get well again. It's a great investment in yourself even if you have to pay 'out of pocket'. (article #87)

    4. *Optimal Relationships for More Evolved People* can help you get back into the flow of life (article #66)

    5. When your energy has improved, use the Facilitated ADC technique to optimally detect your wife's presence (article #9)

### Q#3: My church says the timing of our death is preordained. What do you think?

A#3: Some religious denominations, especially those that see 'God' as controlling every detail, teach this. My thoughts about this view …

1. 'Death' is just the demise of the earthly form which is much less than 1% of who and what you are. In the grand scheme of things, **when** you drop your body is as inconsequential as when you shift from wearing a winter coat to a spring jacket.

2. You are not separate from The Source. Ideally, both you, She, and your spiritual support team determine the timing.

3. If the timing of your passing is totally predetermined, where is the room for free will? And why bother to optimally care for yourself if you are destined to die at a young age?

All in all, that statement about preordained timing of bodily death seems to be one of many that have been passed down through generations of preachers, ministers, and priests. Most were well-meaning and just shared what they had been taught. However, in 2022 and beyond, we can consider this and other supposed truths in the light of contemporary evidence and common sense unclouded by dogma and fear.

### Q#4: During their NDEs, many people see a being of light they identify as Jesus. Is that true for people of other religions?

A#4: A person's earthly beliefs may carry over into their NDE. Christians may initially report that "It's Jesus!" Later, some still feel that is accurate while others realize it is an angel, guide, or The Light. Buddhists may at first perceive The Buddha, and so on for various religions. A unitive model considers that a highly evolved consciousness spoke through great teachers of different times and religions. In that sense, the outward image perceived isn't so important as the love, wisdom, peace, and hope conveyed.

### Q#5: The church I grew up in doesn't make sense to me anymore. They still preach about hell and fearing God.

## Enlightened Religious / Spiritual Teachings

***They are prejudiced toward gays and people of other religions. What more enlightened churches do you recommend?***

A#5: Kudos for recognizing that you have evolved beyond that. Some people may need that strict kind of 'act right or suffer' motivation. During my masters training as a clinical psychologist, I was taught that borderline mentally ill people sometimes prefer fear-based denominations because of the structure and simplicity. It's better to be a well-behaved fundamentalist than a violent alcoholic, wife beater, excessive gambler, or child abuser.

*What kind of people attend* the church can be a bigger factor than the specific religion or denomination. Which ones appeal the most to you? Is their primary focus on being open-minded, open-hearted, respecting diversity, and lovingly serving others? I agree with the saying: 'Truth is one, paths are many.'

I grew up in a Lutheran church and attended a Methodist theological school. Later in life, my dad was Catholic, my brother Baptist, and my mom a 'none'. Over the last 40 years, I've found the following approaches to be quite helpful: Unity, Unitarian-Universalist, Centers for Positive Living, United Church of Christ (UCC), Christian Science, Buddhism, Hinduism, Sufism, and Native American. I'm sure there are other excellent groups that I've not had the time to enjoy. I enjoy attending a variety of different churches and spiritual centers.

Most importantly, nurture a personal relationship with your inner self and Higher Power. Talk with The One via prayer and listen with meditation. Spend time in nature, serve others, learn more about the greater reality, and use centering practices that quiet your brain. Over time, *or perhaps very quickly,* all this can help you do what you came here to do and enjoy the ride.

**Q#6: Some churches say it's better to get buried than cremated. Is the soul affected by how the prior body is handled?**

A#6: Once again, misconceptions and inaccurate teachings can create fear and confusion. *The Bible* doesn't comment on the best way to handle bodies after death. It mentions burial and cremation for people who were in and out of favor with 'God'.

What happens to a person's body after passing is of *no long-term consequence* in the afterlife. Think about it…the earth-suits of some people drown and their no longer needed earthly forms are eaten by fish. The bodies of some astronauts were blown to tiny bits during a space explosion. And so on. If you oversaw the Universe, would you let these different ways of the body dying interfere with the afterlife experience?

Please notice that I didn't say 'the people drowned' or 'the astronauts were blown to tiny bits'. Just their outer shells perished, and **that's a very important distinction.**

Whether the physical body is buried or cremated may seem like a big deal to loved ones on earth who can't see life's big picture. But to those who know more about the greater reality, it *matters very little*. If cremated, *what happens to the ashes* is likewise of little consequence. Some store them in urns for many years while others sprinkle them in nature so the minerals support plant growth. Recently, a recomposing process allows breakdown of a body to usable soil in six to eight weeks. It's less impactful to our planet from pollution and climate-change perspectives.

A few days before my dad changed worlds, I asked if he still wanted 'his' ashes sprinkled in the mountains and ocean. He said, 'I don't care what you do with them. You can put them in the trashcan for all I care.' Dad wasn't depressed or being rude; *he was just that detached from the body* that took him from womb to tomb, but soon wouldn't be needed.

Note: Some spiritual traditions encourage waiting at least three days before a body is buried or cremated. Why? To ensure that the energy / soul is fully detached from the earthly vehicle. This may or may not be needed depending on the PMP's evolution. However, it's not a bad idea to be cautious about this when possible. Waiting three days also gives earth-bound loved ones a chance to prepare for final handling of the earthly shell.

# QUESTION SECTION #10: THE GREATER REALITY

The term *greater reality* describes the totality of life. Estimates are that the average material person's senses detect less than 1% of all that really exists. As such, it's as though you have been looking at life through a tiny pinhole. No wonder so much doesn't make sense!

**There are degrees or levels of knowing about the greater reality.** An intellectualized and superficial knowing about the nature of reality won't take you very far when faced with tough challenges. However, *a deep and internalized knowledge* – that often requires searching and struggling to develop – can inspire and guide how you live. As Maya Angelou and Oprah Winfrey taught, 'When you know better, you do better.'

I use the terms *awakening* and *becoming enlightened* to describe becoming more aware of the greater reality. (I use the present participle form of those verbs to remind myself and others that expanding one's consciousness is an ongoing process.) Other ways to say this include: seeing the light, perceiving the big picture of life, and viewing life with spiritual as well as physical eyes.

I hope this book helps you better comprehend the greater reality and your vital role in it. Doing so will bless yourself and others.

Knowing *'The Great News'* is a huge part of glimpsing more of the big picture of life, so I'll list It again...

## *'The Great News'*

1. continue to live after bodily death, and may be living in parallel realities now.

2. do not really lose 'departed' loved ones and can interact with them again.

3. are integral, infinite, eternal, and beloved parts of Source Energy / Creator.

4. receive assistance / guidance from angels, guides, master teachers, and evolved energies.

5. are sacredly interconnected with all people, animals, and nature.

6. have special purposes for being on this planet at this time.

7. have everything you need to survive and even thrive during this earthly adventure.

8. possess a magnificent body that, when cared for, can optimize your earthly experience.

9. can find meaning and trust the timing behind life's biggest changes such as death.

10. co-create how heavenly / hellish your life feels by your thoughts, words and deeds.

11. can find silver linings and opportunities for growth and service amidst challenges.

12. can likely use SoulPhone technology in the future for communication with postmaterial loved ones and luminaries who can help us heal our world.

## Articles
*#17 Internalizing Your Spiritually Transformative Experiences*

*#20 Revisit Your 'Mystical' Experiences*

*#25 Pre-Birth Planning: Did I REALLY Choose All This?*

*#68 The Big Picture of Life*

*#72 Greater Reality Living*

*#74 Is Your Life Unfolding Perfectly?*

*#76 Twelve Experiences, Many Lessons*

*#80 Why Are You on Earth? SAGE Training*

*#100 Enlightenment*

*#101 When Reaching a Fork in Your Life's Road*

**Books:** *Greater Reality Living, The Big Picture of Life*

**Audio Programs:** *Pre-Birth Planning; Past Life Regression; Holistic Breathing; Ask Your Soul, G.O.D. and Angels*

**Q#1: I love your books but may always have some doubt about life after death. I am about 95% sure, but even a small doubt can seem large sometimes. Any suggestions on how to get to 100%?**

A#1: Your 95% degree of certainty is very good. Let's face it, transitioning to the next phase of life is the biggest trip any of us will take. Many people get nervous about visiting another country so it's normal to have some trepidation about changing worlds. Some channeled information puts it this way: recall how you feel before jumping into a cool pool of water on a warm summer day. You know there will be an initial chill so there's some hesitancy. But soon it feels great. Dropping the body may be like that for some people.

Based on your question, you are likely a more evolved person. That means you have been 'born' and 'died' many times. As such, your inner knowing will kick in when it's time to move on from this time-space slice of life. Take heart at the inspiring words of Helen Keller: *'Death is no more than passing from one room into another. But there's a difference for me, you know. Because in that other room I shall be able to see again.'*

People who are paralyzed will be able to walk robustly. People who are deaf will be able to hear well again. Those with severe physical and emotional wounds will be whole. Focusing on those and other wonderful upsides can assist your understandable concern.

To move toward 100% certainty, I recommend:

1. Pray and intend to know more deeply that death is not a 'good-bye', just a 'see you later'. Meditate and use centering practices to quiet your over-analytical brain that thinks only what it can sense is real. (articles #39, 51, 77)

2. Review the scientific, clinical, and firsthand experience evidence for afterlife. (articles #1, 60, and the *Soul Proof* and *The Afterlife Evidence* books)

3. Read *Greater Reality Living* and take action steps to internalize *'The Great News'* that life continues after death.

4. Have an evidential medium session to boost your certainty about survival of consciousness after bodily death. It's highly impressive to receive *one or more specific bits of information* that only you and a postmaterial loved one would know. Have someone else schedule your appointment so there's no way the medium could research you beforehand. However, by definition, genuine mediums don't need to and wouldn't do that. (article #6)

5. *Use the Facilitated ADC technique* to experience contact with loved ones who have changed worlds. These personal visits can amplify your knowing. (article #9)

6. Stay updated on the SoulPhone Project and use the technology once it's available. If that doesn't convince you, nothing will. (article #35)

**Q#2: If I planned important details before coming to earth, wouldn't I also have planned about finances? I don't want to get rich, I just want to get by but that can be difficult in such a turbulent place.**

A#2: There are several sides to my answer...

1. People with less evolved energies – AKA 'beginner souls' – may not have adequately planned for financial abundance before coming to earth. Their immaturity and ignoring wise counsel could be underlying causes. Or they may have planned well before coming to earth but didn't carry through at key points.

2. People with intermediate to advanced energies / consciousness often aren't very materialistic. They 'seek first the kingdom of God' and know their needs will be met.

3. There's also the aspect of 'ask and you shall receive' and 'as you think, so shall you be'. You "just want to get by" so that could shape what you are experiencing. Maybe you are now ready to enjoy more financial abundance and all the accompanying benefits for you and others.

4. People with advanced energies may actually plan to be poor for the accompanying lessons and benefits. Experiencing poverty can increase their compassion and activism for others. If this sounds too strange, consider the words of Elizabeth Kubler-Ross MD who reported a channeled message from a postmaterial person. To paraphrase, the person said, 'When I return to earth, I'm going to be a child who starves to death.' Dr. Ross replied, 'What kind of nut would ever choose that?' The person said, 'But, Elisabeth, it would enhance my compassion so much!'

5. Some people may need to struggle financially *for karmic reasons*. They may have been a thief or cruel lord in another time / space scenario. As such, they decided to suffer for a while in this one to learn important lessons about stealing and mistreating others. (article #65)

6. People may have planned for financial abundance during this earthly experience, but were negatively impacted by *limiting teachings* during their youth. Four common erroneous lessons about prosperity are:

   a. 'Money is the root of all evil'. Actually, the full context is that an *excessive love of or attachment to* money can lead to problems.

b. 'Your prosperity causes others to suffer'. In reality, having abundance allows you to help others more.

c. 'Having lots of money makes you a bad person.' I've met some wealthy people who were very awakened and helped others a lot. So, we can throw that one out.

d. 'It's easier for a camel to pass through the eye of a needle than for a rich man to enter the kingdom of God.' Like (c), having financial abundance is just one factor that determines whether a person leads a purpose-focused life.

7. Earlier in my life, I would have agreed with your description of earth as being *a turbulent place*. I now view it as *an exquisite place* for loving service, adventure, growth, and enjoyment. Our brains and minds are like computers programmed by our predominant thoughts. Greater reality living can expand every aspect of your earthly experience including financial abundance.

To access your inner wisdom about how to improve your prosperity, use the *Ask Your Soul, G.O.D. and Angels* audio session.

**Q#3: Mark, I am really struggling with spirituality at the moment. There is so much suffering on earth that sometimes spiritual inspirations seem like a bunch of bull crap.**

A#3: I've felt that way at times in the past, and others have shared their disillusions as they journeyed along the spiritual path. Although it may not seem like it, *struggling is actually a good thing*. It **can** help you understand more about life and build spiritual muscles – key reasons why people visit a place like earth. I emphasized the word 'can' because *it is your choice* whether you:

1. Remember you are an infinite being in a totally supportive universe who can always find silver linings to adversity, or

2. Forget who you really are and respond like a helpless victim in a cruel and chaotic world. This approach to life is lovingly called being **a spiritually amnesic thumb sucker.** (That phrase may sound too harsh, but at least one person credits her spiritual awakening to hearing it. Interesting how nearly any stimulus can be the final straw to realization when we are ready.)

This book is designed to help you remember #1 and live in alignment with that great news.

**Q#4: Why all the negativity and violence here on earth? Why do we need you and others to explain about life? Why don't we already know it for ourselves? And why do we grieve so much when someone dies?**

A#4: Wow, way to pack in the questions. Here are my short answers...

1. Earth is a school designed for beginners to learn and grow, and more advanced people / souls to further evolve and serve. Just as in school, some people earn poor grades and others get on the honor roll. Everyone learns their particular set of lessons. Experiencing negativity and violence *provides a contrast that* **can** help you choose love, peace, and harmony. The word 'can' is emphasized because how you react to adversity is your choice. Facing *apparent* challenges and loss can make you better or bitter. (By now, hopefully you understand why I use the word 'apparent'.)

2. Teachers like me help remind people what they already know. The knowledge is within, but it's easy to forget when surrounded by so much fear, misinformation, excessive focus on materialism, and other lower-energy factors. Potential distractions abound that

can cause people to forget what is most important and how to optimally live. I and others are honored to serve this function. Teaching is also a great way to learn lessons at a higher level.

3. Even when you are awakening to the greater reality, a certain amount of grieving is normal. It shows how much you love the person or pet who transitioned from earth. A deep internalized *knowledge that life and love continue lightens that grief, but doesn't take it away completely.* One key to lessening grief is to use the A.R.T. (Appreciate, Realize, Transform) technique. (article #41)

**Q#5: I have been a follower of yours for several years and value your input. I grew up in a Christian home and graduated from a Christian college. So it has been hard to let go of old religious dogma and accept my new spiritual views. Four years before my husband passed on, I had a spiritual awakening. I told him and two dear friends: "Something is happening to me. I don't know what it is but I know it is good". In the last two years, my husband, mother, and father crossed over. My son and his wife had a stillborn child and my dear dog died.**

**Without my awakening, I don't think I could have gotten through all that. Now I feel that I am supposed to help others, but I'm not sure how. Thank you for any input.**

A#5: Like you, I struggled after attending a dogmatic church for several years. See article #83 to learn about my synthesis of spiritual views and relationship with Jesus.

Your story is a perfect example of how to optimally respond to *seeming* tragedies and losses. (I say 'seeming' because we don't really lose dear ones.) That entire scenario is, in the most absolute understanding of life, **a transient virtual reality experience**. Your dear ones agreed to use part of their energy to play roles and make it seem so real.

It's like the children's song: 'Row, row, row your boat, gently down the stream. Merrily, merrily, merrily, merrily, life is but a dream.'

Now you have awakened from fearful teachings that can create horrible beliefs about life. Your *spiritually transformative experience* before your loved ones transitioned from earth prepared you to respond as well as you have. (article #17) Kudos for your desire to help others now. To access your inner guidance about how you might best do that, see articles #21 and 71.

# Question Section #11: The Afterlife

The afterlife isn't the same for all people since it is shaped by your level of consciousness and religious beliefs you've acquired. The quality of your next phase of life also depends upon your goals: what you want to learn and how you desire to grow. Your afterlife is also affected by your predominant thoughts, words, and deeds. If your time on earth was mostly loving, peaceful, and joyful, your afterlife experience will likely be much the same. You take to the afterlife all you learned while living on earth. If you were a rocket scientist on earth, you can remember that knowledge and go from there.

*A caveat*: It's fine to learn about other planes of consciousness, but I encourage you to live fully in this one. One of the most unbalanced and unhappy people I've met spent a lot of time learning about past lives. She had thick journals of notes and drawings about these. Looking back, I'm thankful for her teaching about the importance of the here and now.

## Articles
*#42 What Is the Afterlife for Evil Doers Like?*

*#45 The Life Review Technique: How Would Yours Feel Today?*

*#98 Life Between Lives*

*#100 Enlightenment*

**Books:** *Soul Proof, The Eleven Questions*

**Audio Programs:** *Ask Your Soul, G. O.D., and Angels; Life Review Technique; Facilitated ADC Technique*

**Q#1: Will I really be with my loved ones after I die? If so, how soon after my death? Can I stay with them for a long time or just for a few moments?**

A#1: Clinical data about after death reunions comes from near death experience reports, after death communications, evidential medium input, and Life Between Lives(R) sessions. All of these sources report the *possibility* of visiting loved ones after bodily death. I say 'possibility' because reunions only occur if both parties want that.

Regarding *how soon* such visits might occur, that may depend on several factors:

    1. Do the people who want to visit have beginner, intermediate, or advanced energies?

    2. What was the physical and mental state of the 'recently deceased'? Healthy, joyful, and peaceful? Or very ill, depressed, and distraught?

    3. *How* did the recent person pass on? Peacefully after a long illness so she had time to prepare before changing worlds while surrounded by loved ones? Or unexpectedly and violently so those positives didn't happen?

    4. What are the goals and intentions of both people? To meet as soon as possible or let the recently arrived PMP rest, recharge, and reorient first?

As for the *duration* of your visit, that could also vary depending on a number of variables. It might be as simple as how long you both want and need to be together. One of you may have other priorities to attend to that limit the length of your visit. However, if multilocation is indeed operative, you could visit and attend to other tasks at the same time.

**Q#2: There seem to be different views about what the afterlife is like.**

A#2: This is partly because the afterlife is a reflection of the person's consciousness / energy. Everyone is unique and so is the reality they have co-created. We create the quality and nature of the next phase of life by our awareness, past, personality, and intentions at the time of passing.

Another reason for different views about the afterlife is that reports by authors, mediums, and researchers are based on what they experienced or observed. They may be like the blind men describing what an elephant is like since, given its size, they each can only study part of it. Their answers may be correct for a subset of people, but not for everyone. As such, their descriptions of the afterlife shouldn't be mistaken as representing what it's like for everyone.

**Q#3: My beloved wife changed worlds – I love that way of putting it – two years ago. Can she see what I'm doing? How about when I am ready for a new relationship and intimacy?**

A#3: Postmaterial persons can likely perceive more than material persons because their senses aren't limited by an earthly brain that filters out so much of reality. Your wife's consciousness is nonlocal, that is, not impeded by space or time

Your questions about intimacy in a new relationship are common. Can postmaterial loved ones see you having sex? Those who *could* see that wouldn't disrespect your privacy, and those who *want to* aren't able to.

She likely can see you – *especially if you have continued a close relationship* – but she won't infringe upon your privacy. Those on 'the other side' who **could** observe intimacy on earth wouldn't take advantage of that. They only respectfully visit when it's appropriate and timely. Imbalanced PMPs, who may want to be a 'peeping Tom', don't have the ability to do so.

Not only is your wife likely following how you are doing, **she is also rooting you on** to see through the illusion of separateness and death. If you two were that close, you likely are soulmates. I use this term in the sense that we each have 25 or so primary and a larger number of secondary soulmates. So it's not as though your 'one and only' is gone.

**Q#4: Our baby girl recently died. Will she continue to grow as a child on the other side?**

A#4: Your question reflects so much pain and yearning. I am sorry for your sadness and suffering, but glad you are asking great questions so you and others can heal and move forward.

The answer to your question depends on whether you are observing her with brain-induced myopia or from a greater reality perspective. Babies have appeared to progress through developmental stages when observed via ADCs and evidential medium readings. Parents are sometimes comforted by the thought that their baby gets to go through the different stages and not miss out on anything. The postmaterial person – who previously played the role of a baby on earth – can appear that way to comfort the parents.

However, from a more expansive view, your 'baby' is a deathless being of energy / awareness who can manifest in various ways. After moving into a different realm, she can continue having childhood developmental stages, or not, as preferred. If she had visited earth before, she may not be interested in experiencing grade school, junior high, high school, proms, graduation, etc.

(Note: I use the feminine pronoun 'she' even though gender can shift and blend in different time / space scenarios. Reports are that some PMPs retain their prior masculine or feminine emphasis. Others are more androgynous and some may be asexual. Kind of like on earth.)

If you haven't already, I strongly encourage you to visit the *Helping Parents Heal* website and enjoy the wonderful support, networking, and information from their local and on-line groups.

Their *Caring Listeners* will talk with you at no charge and share how they journeyed **FROM** sad, depressed, and suffering *bereaved parents* **TO** happy, enthusiastic, and service-oriented *shining light parents*. They realize their 'departed' child is a shining being who is – or, depending on factors at the time of passing, soon will be – happy, whole, and peaceful. *Caring Listeners* learned how to focus on those higher energies and are honored to help you do the same.

Put another way, the term 'bereaved / shining light' describes *how you can respond after the bodily death of a loved one*. The first word honors the mourning that precedes transformation; the second describes opportunities that await. That shift can occur more quickly after:

1. knowing that bodily death is not an end. (articles #1, 60)

2. having meaningful contact with your postmaterial loved one via an after death communication and / or evidential medium session. (articles #6, 9, 28)

3. using the A.R.T. formula. (article #41)

4. other information discussed in article #82 *Journey from Bereaved to Shining Light.*

This transformation should become much more rapid and complete after SoulPhone sessions are available. (article #35)

### Q#5: *What is the afterlife like for children?*

A#5: To fully understand my answers, it's vital to remember: *they only **appeared** to be children in that particular earthly experience.* Actually, they are timeless beings of consciousness / energy just like you and me. Over time and in different realms, they may have played the role of people with varying ages, gender, sexual orientation, race, religion, etc. As such, they likely have experienced being born and dying many times.

When the body of a child passes on, the seeming horrible tragedy can make it difficult to remember basic information about the nature of reality. It's possible that only part of the soul's energy was appearing as a child. Even if a recently 'departed' soul appears as a child to a medium or during an ADC, they are not limited to that role all the time.

The other 80% or so of their energy may also experience life as an adult, formless being, or Homebody. (The latter term with a capital 'H' refers to the part of a person's energy that never leaves Home / Oneness.) Understanding these distinctions can help you handle life's biggest challenges – even the bodily death of a child – with peace and grace.

My answers to your question may be difficult to grasp since little ones **seem** so vulnerable. The usual illusion of death can amplify when a child changes worlds. But that limited viewpoint does a disservice to the powerful awareness / soul who visited earth for just a short time.

Some people envision nurseries and schools in the next stage of life where children can continue developmental stages similar to those on earth. That has been reported by NDErs, evidential mediums, and clients after Life Between Lives sessions. Perhaps some souls, especially beginner ones, want to continue playing the role of a child even though they are no longer living on earth. Continuing to manifest as a little one in the afterlife might allow healers in training there to practice their childcare skills.

However, my sense is that appearing as a child is often a temporary manifestation to lessen the parents' grief. Later, they may not need or want to see their child in such a limiting way.

As always, what the afterlife experience is like depends on the PMP's level of consciousness and intentions. The bottom lines? You can be assured that children in the afterlife are lovingly cared for and are in good hands. A marvelous array of experiences awaits them. They can enjoy relationships with ancestors and family pets even if they didn't meet while on earth. And you can see them again.

**Q#6: My former husband passed on eight years ago and has stayed in touch by different signs. I remarried five years ago. How will that work after my current husband and I pass on?**

A#6: Oh my, that could be one big celestial cat fight! Seriously, the short answer is that you can spend time with either husband or both. What? First recall the possibility of simultaneous realities. Then realize that relationships in other realms can be quite different from those on earth. You may be able to manifest so part of you is still married to each of them. If that seems too strange or difficult, know that lower-energy emotions such as jealousy and insecurity can be less common in non-earthly dimensions. This is especially the case for those with intermediate to advanced energies.

Your husbands in this earthly experience may have 'tried on' a primary masculine role but mainly manifest more feminine energies. And vice-versa with you. As such, you may be their husband in the next phase of life instead of, or in addition to, their wife. Considering such mind-boggling possibilities can open our minds to the myriad of interesting possibilities.

From the most absolute view of reality, we each are sacredly interconnected and essentially One. Forever is beyond time so there's no end to love and life. As such, there will be plenty of opportunities for the various scenarios your heart and mind desire. This will work out just fine, especially when that is your intention.

**Q#7: I lost my wife two years ago. She was cycling when a driver who was texting hit and killed her. If she can see me and be near me, can she feel my sorrow?**

A#7: Even though it may not seem like it, there is meaning behind the timing and way of her passing. One of the most convincing stories I've heard about this came from a bereaved mother at a *Helping Parents Heal* conference. Her experience, that she described to me right after the session, still gives me goosebumps – *AKA truth bumps* – when I recall it.

I led a *Facilitated ADC* session with several hundred parents and family members. The goal of this technique is to *increase the chances* of meaningful perceptions of loved ones who changed worlds. The mom's intention was to visit with her teenage daughter whose earthly form was killed by a hit-and-run driver. After reaching a deeply relaxed state, she was surprised to see a man who she intuitively knew was the driver. She started to react angrily toward him, but then looked into his eyes. 'All I saw was love and sadness', she said.

As the session proceeded, she came to believe that he, like her daughter, was a primary soulmate. They all agreed, **out of love**, to experience a brief earthly experience in which the daughter's body might be killed by this man. Why? Because the mom had a history of remaining in spiritual amnesia when she visited places of learning like earth. The souls / energies of the daughter and man agreed to help the mom wake up in this earthly incarnation so she could complete her curricula and share her greatest gifts.

It worked because the mom had a spiritually transformative experience after the 'accident'. She became a force for good on our planet, learned important lessons, and fulfilled her reasons for being here. The mom realized that she was at least partly responsible for her daughter's passing. (I say *partly* because her daughter also likely benefited from the mode and timing of her seemingly premature passing.)

The mom also saw that playing this role broke the human heart of the driver and he died soon afterwards. But they all knew it was a relative illusion lasting only a blink of an eye that could yield much growth and service. As such, they volunteered to have that brief virtual reality experience that appeared, from a limited human view, to be a horrible and random accident.

I hope her experience helps you fathom the depth of love, meaning, design, and timing behind ways of passing on that **seem** to be senselessly tragic and random. Returning to your question, depending on her level of consciousness and the strength of your connection, your wife may know you are sad. However, *she may not feel sad because she knows 'The Great News'* that:

1. Life and love continue after bodily death.

2. Everyone is part of Source and sacredly interconnected with all of life right now.

3. You two can have contact with each other now and when you pass on.

4. This earthly experience lasts just a nanosecond in the span of eternity.

5. Her bodily death, while tragic from a limited earthly perspective, was her ticket back Home. She was ready to graduate from earth school and needed a way to leave earth.

For all those reasons, your wife is probably not sorrowful when you are sad. She is rooting you on to remember life's big picture and focus on higher-energy emotions and ways of being. If you can adopt this view of life, you will increasingly grow, serve others, and enjoy life again.

**Q#8: I've heard that if we experienced trauma on earth, we're provided with a healing shower after passing on. If this is true, why do some people carry past life traumas into their current time on earth?**

A#8: Thanks for that great question. Healing showers are described as *washing away lower-energy emotions* – fear, pain, anger, hopelessness, etc. – that accumulated on earth. Then *higher-energy emotions* – peace, joy, love, etc. – are transmitted to help recently arrived persons recharge, remember, and heal. This allows them to be more clear and vital while entering the next phase of life.

However, healing showers may provide only *a temporary release and recharge* to allow the newly 'deceased' person to optimally enjoy reunions and get reoriented. That doesn't provide **complete and lasting** healing and transformation. If that were so, it would:

1. Negate growth and learning. Why work on earth if everything is totally and forever made perfect after bodily death by a healing shower?

2. Bypass free will and personal responsibility. Creator is not in the business of making robots. Perhaps retaining some past life trauma is part of that soul's plan to evolve and serve.

3. Some people may not be ready to re-enter the mainstream of life. A mass murderer, for example, may need extensive sleep and rehab before beginning the healing process.

The degree to which recently arrived postmaterial persons benefit from healing showers is probably dependent upon their state of consciousness. More advanced souls, who only need a healing sponge bath, can quickly internalize the higher energies. Beginners might be in shock, reject the revitalization, and need a very long healing soak.

### Q#9: Do we start each earthly experience refreshed?

A#9: I used to work in a hospital with pediatric and maternity wards. Based on being around many babies and children – both professionally and personally – it seems that most new arrivals to earth arrive relatively refreshed. Babies are usually quite energized and blissful. In addition, they may still remember who they are, why they're here, and Who walks beside them always.

However, that does not appear to always be the case. Some beginner souls / people may make impulsive choices in their pre-birth planning. They may choose poor body-brain matches that aren't optimal for their level of consciousness. Others may choose family members and geographical place of origin in cavalier ways. These factors can result in lower chi / life force energy, imbalances, illness, birth defects, carry over of lower-energies, ongoing spiritual amnesia, and not fulfilling their purposes on earth.

I'm not at all suggesting that all congenital anomalies, pediatric illnesses, and severe childhood injuries are the result of not arriving to earth refreshed. Those challenges could be chosen by the energy / soul within for spiritual growth, adventures, and service to others. An account of an amazing young man illustrates why people might choose adversity early in life. At age eight, Joshua Dixon was attacked by two pit bulls and his face was basically torn off. At the age of 18 – and 59 surgeries later – he started art school.

Looking back at the attack, he stated: "I wouldn't take it back. I've met so many people that a regular person wouldn't have met in a lifetime." Joshua's dream is to become an art therapist and help others recover from crises. He is one of my heroes and teachers. Could it be that he volunteered to go through this horrible tragedy, in part, so his story could inspire others?

**Q#10: I've read stories of people bringing phobias or health conditions into this life that seem to be a direct result of an experience / trauma from a previous life.**

A#10: Yes, I've experienced this with patients who required past life regression therapy to release the underlying causes. That carryover may be due to:

1. severe emotional and / or physical trauma.

2. sudden and unexpected bodily death.

3. volunteering to have those symptoms so fledgling caregivers can practice on them.

4. willingness to provide a clinical case that contributes to the afterlife evidence.

**Q#11: Some 'astral travel' authors say we bring our state of consciousness with us when our body dies. If we are ignorant on earth, we don't magically become wise and enlightened in the next realm. If that is the case, I want to develop myself and be around higher souls now. Wouldn't that benefit me now and in the afterlife?**

A#11. I agree with those authors and applaud your plan. While living on earth, it's tough to remember the big picture of life and work on oneself. But doing so is a huge part of creating the greatest life you have envisioned here and in the hereafter. As the old saying goes, *wherever you go, there you are.* Another motivating thought is: 'Do you want to carry your dirty earthly laundry into your next phase of life?' Of course not.

Bravo for recognizing that refining yourself holistically and spending time with kindred spirits can improve your quality of life on earth and beyond. To learn more, see articles #12 and 66.

**Q#12: Can I keep my earthly name after crossing over?**

A#12: My sense is you can continue to use that name, especially when interacting with someone you knew on earth. But that might got confusing if you've had many experiences with the same souls while playing different roles. Perhaps you have *an overarching name* that captures your essence, AND also can keep your current one. Enhanced communication in nonearthly realms – via telepathy and inner knowing, for example – might make permanent names less important.

Whatever the case, keep asking great questions and searching for meaningful and sensible answers. Life is so vast and magnificent. The more I learn about it, the more grateful and safe I feel. Increasingly, I understand William Blake's awe of seeing 'a world in a grain of sand.'

# QUESTION SECTION #12: PARALLEL REALITIES

Many years ago, a Native American teacher showed me a portrait of a brave: above his head was a bear, pine trees, eagle, moon, and stars. He asked what message I got from this artwork. I said it seemed to teach that people can have *different experiences at the same time* even though it seems we are limited to this earthly one. Synonyms for 'parallel realities' are *multilocation* and *simultaneous experiences*.

I've read and re-read the books written by Michael Newton PhD about the nature of reality during life between lives. Many Life Between Lives clients have similarly and independently reported that **only about 20% of one's life-force is needed for an earthly experience**. The rest of one's energy can allow experiencing life from other observation points and / or remaining merged with the One. Later, I learned of high energy physicists such as David Deutsch PhD whose mathematical models support the possibility of multilocation.

This topic also suggests that *this seemingly solid, separate, and short earthly experience may be more of a virtual reality (VR) experience than you might imagine*. In this model of reality, your consciousness is visiting other times and places using super-enhanced technology versus 'really' being in each experience. Using VR technology is also a great demonstration that your human senses are less reliable than you might think. I recently used VR for the first time and was amazed at how real it all seemed even though I knew it was 'just' a technology-enabled experience.

**Articles**
*#34 Reincarnation: Evidence of Cyclical Life Experiences*

*#75 Multilocation / Parallel Realities / Simultaneous Experiences*

**Books:** *Greater Reality Living*

**Audio Programs:** The *Past Life Regression* technique can be used to explore other time-space scenarios. Other techniques to expand your perceptions about life include *Facilitated ADC, Pre-Birth Planning,* and *Ask Your Soul, G. O.D., and Angels*

**Q#1: As a rule, my dreams are jumbled and make no sense. But in a recent dream, I was somewhere else and people were trying to communicate something of importance to me. I felt like I really went somewhere in the past! What is 'The Pitstick Perspective' about this?**

A#1: 'The Pitstick perspective'… I like that, but be sure to primarily develop and trust your own perspective. In general, dreams can be categorized as a: (1) review, perhaps in bizarre form, of recent events on earth; (2) visit with / learning from PMPs, soulmates, angels, guides, and master teachers; and (3) greater awareness of / accessing parallel realties.

Vivid and meaningful dreams occur most often for me around 3AM. I keep a notepad and pen on my bedside table to capture important information and insights. Dream ADCs, that I have quite often with postmaterial loved ones, are an example of #2 above. Those often leave a deep peace and certainty that contact with 'departed' dear ones really occurred. (article #28)

Even though most humans think about time as being linear / chronological, that may be limited or erroneous. Some evidence indicates that the past, present, and future are all happening simultaneously. As such, what seem like 'past lives' may actually be parallel multi-dimensional experiences. To get an expanded sense of this, watch the scene at 'the Past Lives Pavilion' in the wonderful movie *Defending Your Life*.

**Q#2: My question is about reincarnation. Do we have a choice to stay in 'spirit world' or must we leave our loved ones and return to earth? I ask because maybe a person hasn't fulfilled God's plan for them.**

A#2: Some people / souls may choose to not come back to earth for a number of reasons. Others recognize the benefits of periodically returning to a place where they seem to be solid, separate, and mortal. By now, you know that not all of you / your soul's energy may be invested in one earthly experience. Part of your essence may experience life from another time / place, and part might never leave Home / 'spirit world'.

As for not fulfilling God's plan, *planning one's missions is ideally a joint effort* between you, One Mind, and higher-energy assistants. If a separate and dictatorial 'God' planned everything, people would be puppets. However, evidence suggests that we each are integral parts of the One. From that perspective, then, G.O.D. does plan everything since It is all and is in all.

**Q#3: If deceased family members are watching over us, how can they reincarnate? They can't be both on earth and in heaven, can they?**

A#3: It's unlikely that your loved ones would return to earth before you pass on. During my past life regression therapy training with Brian Weiss MD, I learned that – on average – people reincarnate after 150 earth-years from the time of their passing. After bodily death, new arrivals recharge, reorient, have reunions, learn, enjoy different experiences, and plan their next adventures before having the next formed or formless incarnation with that part of their energy. From a dualistic perspective, all that takes time. (article #34)

This gets even more interesting when considering the potential for multilocation / parallel realities. In that sense, the energy / consciousness of your loved ones can be watching over you even if they have returned to a place like earth. (article #75) Given both factors, I wouldn't worry that praying for their assistance and guidance will interfere with their optimal progress.

They, like you, are very powerful, capable, and creative.

**Q#4: After I pass on, will I reunite with my departed wife and son? I ask because I hear conflicting stories about reincarnation. What if they are somewhere else when I die?**

A#4: Please see A#3. However, you probably don't have to wait until you cross over to enjoy contact with them. To learn more about how to visit with postmaterial loved ones now, see article #9.

**Q#5: I've had repeated dreams about being with a guy that I've never met while on earth. The dreams seem so very real at the time. Any ideas?**

A#5: Despite the repetition, your dreams may have no meaning. Or they might reflect your idealized version of a man and the kind of relationship you desire. However, given the vivid nature of your recurrent dreams, they could be visits with a soulmate that occur while your body sleeps. You two may know each other in another time / space slice of life but haven't met in this one.

Before you go to sleep, say a prayer / set an intention to communicate with this unknown person. Ask who he is and what messages he brings. It may take some practice to gather more information, but it could be interesting and instructive.

**Q#6: Reincarnation makes so much sense, but when does it all end? I don't see any endgame, just a never-ending cycle of people coming to earth over and over again.**

A#6: My understanding is that *you can choose* to stop visiting earth. You are not forced to take on formed incarnations in which you will likely forget about the big picture of life.

However, would you ask, 'When does it all end?' about reading books, watching movies, taking trips, and enjoying virtual reality experiences? From a greater reality perspective, that is what earthly experiences are: very brief and semi-illusory stories and visits created in your mind. Internalizing *'The Great News'* helps you more fully enjoy the growth, service, and adventures that accompany an earthly incarnation. Yes, you can halt earthly visits, but why limit the depth and variety of your experiences?

Depending on their level of awareness, people come to / pretend to visit earth because:

    1. *Beginner souls* are like preschoolers who need and want to attend classes / have earthly experiences to awaken and learn.

    2. *Those with intermediate energies* find this planet to be a magnificent classroom for learning, and an exquisite opportunity for serving others.

    3. *Advanced beings* know earthly visits can enable more growth and service to others.

4. *Super-evolved beings* may manifest on earth as angels, guides, and master teachers so they can teach, serve, expand love, and raise the energy of this planet.

It's a great set up, especially when you remember who you are, know you are one with Source, release fear, and enjoy the journey.

**Q#7: My attempts at past life regressions seem to be blocked by traumatic events earlier in this time on earth. What can I do about this?**

A#7: Your challenge is fairly common. Solutions for having meaningful past life regressions include...

1. Use the *Holistic Breathing Technique* twice a week for one month. Set an intention to release all blocks that prevent successful regressions and a harmonious life. Continue to use this technique with the frequency described in the Introduction track. (article #38)

2. After one month, add the *Ask Your Soul, G.O.D. and Angels* technique to access your inner wisdom about how to release all blocks including those to past life regressions. (#71)

3. After one month of #2, have a past life regression with a therapist or use my audio product. As discussed in article #102, create an optimal environment beforehand: ensure no interruptions, be fully rested, turn off all electronic devices, no caffeine before the session, etc.

These action steps may result in a meaningful and helpful past life regression for you if, all things considered, that is optimal for you at this time.

# QUESTION SECTION #13: AFTER DEATH COMMUNICATIONS

The term *after death communication* (ADC) describes meaningful contact with a person who has passed on. ADCs may occur via the usual senses or more ethereal ones such as seeing with the mind's eye, telepathically hearing, or inner knowing. Dream ADCs seem very real and lucid while imparting peace and a lasting sense that an actual visit occurred.

In the past, many people didn't share after death communications for fear of being considered weird or crazy. More people are now openly sharing these surprisingly common experiences. According to Dr. Raymond Moody, ADCs have been reported by 25 percent of Americans, 66 percent of widows, and 75 percent of parents whose children have changed worlds. However, when I survey large groups of bereaved parents, nearly all of them indicate they've had one or more contacts with their child.

**Articles**
*#9 Visiting 'Departed' Loved Ones Now*

*#28 After Death Communications*

*#31 What Is a 'Postmaterial Person'?*

**Books:** *Soul Proof, The Afterlife Evidence, The Big Picture of Life*

**Audio Programs:** *Facilitated ADC Technique*

**Q#1: After his baby brother died, my grandson woke up one night and saw a green ball of light floating in the air. He thought he was dreaming until he touched it with his hand. Could that have been a visitation from his brother?**

A#1: Many people have reported seeing multi-colored orbs and photographing them with different cameras, film, and settings. To my knowledge, no clinical or scientific research has been done about these images so I can't make definitive statements. Touching these isn't often reported so perhaps he indeed had an ADC with his brother. I hope your grandson appreciates how lucky he is to have such a wise, loving, and open-minded grandma.

**Q#2: I had a dream and my Mom, who died from lung cancer 3 years ago, was in it. She looked young, glowing, and oozing with LIFE! We talked and she told me I would have a baby boy. I later did give birth to a son. Was that really a visit with her?**

A#2: Your lucid dream, especially with validation about the birth and gender of your baby, could be an actual visit. Those usually stick with people for a lifetime and help them be less fearful about bodily death. Your mom appearing as a young and healthy person is consistent with many ADCs with people whose bodies were ravaged before death. Seeing her as young and oozing with LIFE – *what a great phrase* – is a wonderful gift. See the articles listed above to learn how to regularly communicate with her and other postmaterial loved ones.

**Q#3: A few days after my sister died, strange events started in our house. Lights flickered on and off, the garage door opened and closed several times, and a photo of us fell over. All that happened for a few days for no obvious reason, then didn't happen again. During that time, I felt her around me more strongly. Was that her?**

A#3: It certainly is possible given the combination of unusual events and feeling her presence. If that was her, she sounds like a dynamo! What you described are three of the most common 'non-animal' signs. (A fourth involves books falling off a shelf for no reason.)

I'll share my most amazing experience like this. In 2016, Dr. Gary Schwartz and I agreed in a Skype meeting to collaborate on the SoulPhone Project. Right afterwards, I trimmed my beard in front of the bathroom mirror before taking a shower. When I opened the shower curtain, *the mirror was tilted at a 40 degree angle.* (That's a big tilt!)

I'm very aware and sometimes even overly focused on details. So *I knew* without a doubt that it wasn't tilted before. That heavy mirror is securely hung and had never tilted in 20 years.

I silently asked, "If this is a sign, what message do you bring?" Immediately, a calm and wise voice / thought in my head replied, "We are helping you with your new outreaches." I then thought, "*Who is 'we'?*" Again, an instantaneous answer popped up in a fraction of a second: "Dad and others." I wondered, "Who are the others?" The answer arrived before my thought was completed: "Uncles Milt and Cliff, Aunt June, and both grandmas and grandpas."

Feeling slightly overwhelmed, I incredulously thought, "All my close departed relatives are *really* helping?" The reply was both

## After Death Communications

loving and teasing: "Of course! Are you kidding? We are so proud of our family member who is helping awaken humanity to life's big picture. We are pleased to help in any way we can."

I felt humbled and deeply moved by the experience. **It felt completely true** that my dear family members who had changed worlds would assist and guide me. We were all so close while they were on earth. It makes sense that those bonds would naturally continue after bodily death.

My advice to those who experience what may be signs from post-material loved ones...

1. Take a few deep breaths to calm and center yourself.

2. Ask basic questions such as: "Who are you? What message do you bring?"

3. Listen / feel for subtle and fleeting, but clear and wise responses.

4. If you are comfortable doing so, share your experience with others and consider follow-up action steps.

**Q4: Your messages have been a great help to me since the passing of our son two years ago. He took an overdose of depression medication and left us without warning. During his funeral service, my neighbor saw a grey mist raise up from my son's body. Was that his soul leaving the body? If so, why did it leave so long after the body died?**

A#4: I'm glad my outreaches have helped. Thank you for sharing this interesting event. When the earthly shell perishes, some people linger a bit to make sure their loved ones are OK. They send signs of peace and comfort that may or may not be noticed.

I've seen whitish light emanate from the chest of two patients just as the doctor called their time of death.

The mist may have been a way to remind you and your family that: he loves you, he is alive and well, you will see each other again, he is sorry for overdosing but just couldn't stay on earth anymore, he is happy and at peace and wants you to be the same.

Maybe your son's energy / life force fully detached from his no-longer-needed shell during the service. Perhaps *the timing of that* was so someone with extrasensory abilities would notice and tell you.

If you haven't already, read articles #1, 2, and 4. *Radio Shows* on SoulProof.com provide my views and those of others on topics such as 'Why do children die?' and 'What happens to those who pass on by suicide?' I hope these resources allow you to heal, transform, and share the blessings that always accompany adversity.

**Q#5: My wife passed away unexpectedly six months ago due to necrotizing fasciitis. It was all over in 12 hours. Immediately after, I got signs such as dreams and clocks stopping at the time of her passing. Why is she not coming to me now?**

A#5: I am glad you know she is alive and well in another phase of life. Regarding why she's not been in contact since she first transitioned, several possibilities include:

    1. Her rapid and severe illness might have taken a toll on her life-force. She knew you detected her early signs so now she can focus on healing and recharging. Six months earth-time may not be that long in her new abode.

2. After her initial contacts and knowing you are doing pretty well, she may be helping those with bigger needs.

3. Her lack of contact could be what I call 'a spiritual setup' that you two designed before visiting earth. You agreed because you knew her lack of visits could test your faith and strengthen you. It also caused you to ask this question which will help many people.

**Q#6: A few weeks after my brother passed on, a rare bird kept pecking at the window. It seemed to look right at us and wasn't afraid. Could this have been my brother?**

A#6: Unusual 'animal signs' are often reported after a loved one changes worlds. Those can involve birds, insects, or four-legged animals. However, if indeed it was a sign from your brother, *that doesn't mean he actually is or was that creature.* Here's how several top evidential mediums have explained it to me...

1. Postmaterial loved ones want to send comforting signs they are alive and well.

2. They send energy to a nearby bird, insect, or animal that notices the different energy.

3. A telepathic communication is made so the creature knows what is desired.

4. The animal is glad to help; it enjoys the 'change of pace' and opportunity to help.

5. Loved ones on earth notice the unusual behaviors and may interpret those as signs from a loved one now living in a different part of forever.

**Q#7: I lost my teenage daughter who was born with a debilitating heart defect. She was so pure and beautiful. I tucked her in around 9pm and heard a knock at my door at 11 pm that woke me. I checked on her and found her dead. Could the knock have been a sign from her?**

A#7: It certainly could have been. Given your love and closeness, it makes sense that she would let you know she was moving on to the next phase of life. That knock also could be the first contact in a different but very meaningful relationship with her real self. Read the articles and use the technique listed above to expand that connection.

Our loved ones want to stay in touch and share their exciting new lives. Andy Lee, an evidential medium who was a pediatric RN for 30 years, describes postmaterial children who came to her and asked: 'Why can't others see us like you can?' Some of them suffered with debilitating illnesses for years. After their bodies died, they excitedly asked her, 'Can I ride a bike now? Can I go fishing again?'

Your daughter is now healthy and whole. Higher-energy emotions and ways of being are one key to being on a similar wavelength as her. See article #41 on the A.R.T. technique to focus on higher thoughts: appreciate your time together, realize you will see each other again, and transform as you find and share the silver linings.

**Q#8: My Mum passed on four months ago. The other night, I went to bed and said, "Mum, if you are here, can you make a noise? Drop something, move something, anything would be really nice!" Two minutes later – CRASH and the wardrobe door flew open. A hook had snapped off from the inside of the door and bags fell down. Her answering my request?**

A#8: That's why it's said, "Be careful what you ask for!" Did someone get a picture of your face when that happened? Given the proximity of your request and the crash, it may indeed have been your Mum. If so, she sounds like a powerhouse with a great sense of humor and timing.

Soak that experience up and *let it convince you to your core* that life and love are forever. Tell others so they also feel more comfortable sharing their own experiences.

**Q#9: I think my husband, who died five years ago, prepared me for his passing. The day before he died, a family picture fell down and my car alarm turned on repeatedly. In my dreams that night, I saw him flying peacefully into the sky. Can somebody inform you before they change worlds? Please let me know because I still cry and cry every day.**

A#9: Thank you for your question and implied trust. I've heard other stories similar to yours. Those who are close to moving into the next stage of life can send signs to their loved ones. This can lessen the shock and prepare loved ones for what's to come.

The frequency and intensity of your crying sound excessive given the amount of time since his transition and the experiences you described. I recommend:

1. Read article #3 and take action steps.

2. Read articles #12, 70, 82, 87 and improve your self-care habits. If you are still grieving so deeply after 60 days, schedule a *personalized nutritional healing* visit as described in article #32.

3. Use the *Ask Your Soul, G.O.D., and Angels* technique to access your and their inner wisdom about how to optimally heal.

# QUESTION SECTION #14:
# EVIDENTIAL MEDIUMS

Can extrasensorily gifted persons accurately communicate with 'the deceased'? This question has been asked by many people over time. Scientific studies of evidential mediums replicated at five universities and research centers have affirmatively answered this question.

*Evidential medium* is a term for sensitive persons who can detect those who have passed on. To be considered 'evidential', this ability must be verified by one or more double blind evaluations by a researcher.

Mediums may perceive postmaterial persons (PMPs) via sight (clairvoyance), hearing (clairaudience), feeling (clairsentience) or a combination of these. Some evidential mediums can objectively or outwardly sense PMPs as they do material persons. More often, however, their senses are more subjective or inward. That is, their perceptions seem *more subtle as if coming directly from or through their minds*. This has been described as seeing with the mind's eye, telepathic hearing, or having a strong knowing or feeling.

Some people don't know about the legitimacy of evidential mediums because of abuse by fake ones. Fraudulent mediums may use deception, cold readings, fishing, and other unscrupulous ways to deceive clients. Other mediums provide poor to mediocre results with very general information. Consider, for example, a medium who tells a seventy-year-old sitter that his grandmother has died and loves him very much. That isn't very impressive except to those grasping at straws because of fear of death or so badly wanting to have contact.

Fortunately, certification programs now exist to evaluate mediums under blinded conditions. To learn more, see article #6. A good reading can be a spiritually transformative experience that increases your inner knowing that there is much more to life than meets the eye.

**Articles**
*#6 Evidential Mediums*

**Books:** *Greater Reality Living, Soul Proof*

**Q#1: How can I find a great medium? I've heard that some are fakes while others have genuine gifts.**

A#1: I agree with your assessment. *The Afterlife Experiments* by Gary E. Schwartz PhD discusses this topic and describes university studies evaluating the authenticity of mediums. See article #6 to learn more about finding outstanding ones. I know many of these mediums firsthand and can vouch for their integrity and professionalism.

**Q#2: A medium said my deceased husband is stuck on earth and I want to help him go into the Light. But if he does, will I still be able to communicate with him via a pendulum, dreams, and talking?**

A#2: He may not be so much 'stuck' as 'sticking around', in part, because of the very concerns you mentioned. Your husband doesn't have to move into another realm to have a heavenly life; he might be very happy staying close to you.

As mentioned, the accuracy of mediums can be fake, poor, mediocre, or excellent. As such, I wouldn't put too much stock in what you were told unless you had a medium whose highly specific and accurate abilities have been verified in double-blinded research studies.

If he is indeed 'stuck', you might assist by letting him know you will be OK if he moves on. It's possible that you may perceive him *even better* after he has entered the Light.

### Q#3: How do I know a medium hasn't researched me before a session?

A#3: Have a friend make the appointment and handle payment for your session. Then the medium can have no idea who you are and whom you hope to contact. Good mediums will welcome this anonymous approach. They don't need to research beforehand since they can sense your postmaterial loved ones and relay what they share. Another way to guard against fraud is to use a medium listed in article #6 or who has been vetted by one of the certification methods I mention.

### Q#4: My wife died last year and I am having a tough time. Someone suggested contacting a medium so I really know she is alive. What do you think?

A#4: I think it's a great idea IF you work with a genuine medium. A good reading can make a huge difference in your certainty that life continues after bodily death. You can be like Demi Moore's character in the movie *Ghost* where she sees a penny floating in the air. I encourage you to watch the movie and realize the potential power of receiving a clear sign from your wife. Then see article #6 to learn how to find an evidential medium.

# QUESTION SECTION #15: THE SOULPHONE PROJECT

Gary E. Schwartz PhD is a senior professor at the University of Arizona where he directs the *Laboratory for Advances in Consciousness and Health.* Dr. Schwartz, formerly an assistant professor at Harvard and tenured professor at Yale, has presented more than 450 scientific papers, co-edited 11 academic books, and written 12 books for the general public. (To learn more, visit SoulPhone.com and LACH.Arizona.edu.

He and a team of electrical engineers, software programmers, evidential mediums, and postmaterial collaborators (the A-Team) have worked for 15 years on the SoulPhone Project. The goal is to create practical technology to communicate with PMPs. The first device, the SoulSwitch, currently provides clear evidence that (1) life continues after bodily death, and (2) at least some 'deceased' persons can use the equipment to signal Yes / No answers.

*Official announcements and demonstrations* about this are anticipated to occur in 2022 – 2023 after completion of multi-center studies and attaining minimal response times with the SoulSwitch. As the director of the SoulPhone Foundation and research assistant for the SoulPhone Project, I am very knowledgeable about its wonderful potential benefits for many people and our planet.

## Articles
*#35 The SoulPhone: Who Would You Call?*

*#44 SoulPhone Updates*

*#85 Will the SoulPhone EVER Be Ready?*

**Books:** *Greater Reality Living*

## Q#1: Why is it called 'the SoulPhone' if the first device only provides Yes / No answers?

A#1: The term SoulPhone is an umbrella term for four anticipated devices:

    1. **SoulSwitch™** is needed for #2.

    2. **SoulKeyboard™** should allow **texting and typing with PMPs**. Design and development of this device can begin after a sufficiently accurate and near real-time SoulSwitch is available.

    3. **SoulVoice™** is envisioned to allow **talking to and hearing PMPs**. The goal is to achieve sufficient audio fidelity so continuous speech can be detected and understood.

    4. **SoulVideo™** will hopefully enable seeing PMPs. This visual imaging system may eventually become a 3-D holographic version.

## Q#2: When can people purchase these devices?

A#2: Based on progress to date, eventual use of these devices is likely but not a certainty. The SoulSwitch is still in the research and development (R & D) state. A PMP response time with the switch of ten seconds or less is needed to start SoulKeyboard R & D. If and when the keyboard is ready, that technology will initially be available *only as a service*.

The current thinking is that *SoulPhone Call CentersTM* will be established for texting sessions with PMP loved ones. That level of technology will also allow us to communicate with postmaterial luminaries – inventors, health care experts, optimal leaders, etc. – who want to help us and our world.

Proceeding this way will allow the SoulPhone Project team to ensure security and satisfaction for consumers and the technology. This 'service versus product first' approach will allow improvements to be made after early SoulKeyboard sessions. When conditions are optimal, commercialization of actual devices and / or apps will allow widespread use of the technology. Downloadable apps are envisioned for a monthly fee on 'Smart' devices.

### Q#3: Is it right to make a profit from this spiritual enterprise? Will SoulPhone devices be available for everyone for free?

A#3: Some think it should be free to everyone, but a number of people have contributed tremendous amounts of time to this project. For example, I have put in at least 40 hours per week for six years without being paid a penny.

Others have donated small to large amounts of money to advance R & D of this technology. Additional funds are needed to move forward as quickly and optimally as possible. Enormous costs are involved for equipment, software development, electrical engineers, and consultants. If there is no profit, who pays for all this?

Creating SoulPhone devices and making services and devices widely available will require a well-run business. The costs of forming and running this interdimensional business are tremendous.

Planning, design, manufacturing, legal protection, marketing, and customer service will all be needed. Each of these facets incur tremendous costs. Do people expect Smart devices to be free to everyone? Our goal is for SoulPhone services and devices to be available at a reasonable price, that is, to anyone who can afford a cellphone. We will also make some pro bono sessions available.

**Q#4: I thought those who have crossed over communicate mentally versus verbally. If that is true, how would the SoulAudio device work? Also, regarding the SoulVideo device, how would we see our loved ones if they no longer have a physical body?**

A#4: There are lots of opinions about how postmaterial persons communicate and appear. These beliefs come from:

1. Ancient and heavily altered religious texts

2. Firsthand experiences during after death communications, for example, 'She spoke to me telepathically.'

3. Input from medium readings such as 'Your loved one appears as multicolored light.'

However, these snippets from individual perspectives may not accurately reflect how things really work in the next realm. Depending on whether the postmaterial person has low or high energies / consciousness, there may be a wide range of what they can do. Based upon experiments to date with the A-Team, we know that PMPs can communicate and be detected in a variety of ways. SoulPhone technology should allow us to tap into those.

For example, PMPs may signal their presence differently depending upon whom they wish to interact with. They may subtly communicate with those who hear with 'their mind's ear' and can't take too much of a shock. Or they may appear in solid physical form with those who can sense and handle their visual image. If that might be too much too soon, they may appear in more gauzy form, as a fleeting glimpse, or in 'the mind's eye'.

Basic scientific research conducted by Dr. Schwartz and his team at the University of Arizona lab indicates that postmaterial people can speak outwardly in ways that can be detected by sensing instruments. Other experiments have shown that PMPs have, or can have if desired, sufficient density / physicality to slow the speed of light and cause air disturbances in a sealed environment.

Stay tuned to learn how this fledging science fiction-sounding beginning becomes a scientific fact yielding available technology. To learn more, visit SoulPhone.com.

### Q#5: Before donating, how can I be sure the SoulPhone Project is on the up and up?

A#5: Kudos for being skeptical and ensuring your money is well spent. The SoulPhone Foundation is a 501c3 (charitable tax-exempt organization) registered with the IRS. Donations to the SoulPhone Foundation can be tax-deductible. The Federal Identification Number (FIN) is: 81-4529985. To learn more, visit *Membership and Donations / Get Involved* at SoulPhone.com.

You can also see a recent letter from the President and CEO of the University of Arizona Foundation thanking the SoulPhone Foundation for a recent large donation. Those funds paid for research and operational costs at the *Laboratory for Advances in Consciousness and Health* for two years.

These days, people don't know who to trust and what to believe. Some show little regard about making factual statements that can be trusted. See Dr. Schwartz's book *Extraordinary Claims Require Extraordinary Evidence: The Science and Ethics of Truth Seeking and Truth Abuse.* His FACT method can help you distinguish between false statements versus what is most probably true based on the preponderance of evidence.

# Part 2: Tough Challenges While on Earth

# QUESTION SECTION #16: WHY WOULD 'GOD' ALLOW ___?

I am often asked questions that begin with those four words. This is very understandable given: (1) the degree of suffering on our planet, and (2) a supposed Higher Power that is all knowing, all loving, and all powerful.

Some of these questions would be heart-breaking and difficult / impossible to answer without a solid grasp of the big picture of life. For example, many parents have asked, 'Why did God take my child?' Others ask, 'Why did God take my husband from me?' Some people then feel guilty about questioning. Matters are made even worse if their belief system includes the possibility of a fiery eternal hell.

Might their doubt and anger toward Creator be *the final straw* that leads them to false beliefs that they could spend eternity with 'the devil'?

Misunderstandings about E.L.G.O.D. create much needless suffering, confusion, and hopelessness. Fortunately, evidence-based contemporary understandings now allow these questions to be answered sensibly and accurately.

### Articles
*#13 What is G.O.D. Really Like?*

*#15 The True Nature of Humans*

*#25 Pre-Birth Planning: Did I REALLY Choose All This?*

*#78 Why Did God Take My Loved One?*

*#89 My Prayers*

*#100 Enlightenment*

**Books:** *Soul Proof, The Big Picture of Life, The Eleven Questions*

**Audio Programs:** *Ask Your Soul, G. O.D., and Angels*

## Q#1: Why would God allow so much pain and suffering on earth?

A#1: During theology school, I talked with a man who had attended church every week, taught Sunday School, studied the Bible, and had a great relationship with his understanding of 'God'. Then his young son died tragically. This man became bitter and scoffed at any notion of a loving and powerful Higher Power. He wondered why he was being punished and why God took his child.

Upon seeing and feeling his pain and despair, I initially felt anger toward Creator. What kind of world is this where little children die and their loved ones suffer so deeply? Asleep at the wheel again, Omnipresent, Omnipotent, and Omniscient One?

And then I remembered newer and more sensible images of Source that have emerged from many firsthand experiences and contemporary clinical evidence. The Ground of All Being is not a huge guy in the sky who controls all events: "I'll smite this one, save this one, a miracle for her, early death for him."

One Mind is, rather, a supremely loving intelligence / energy that creates and sustains all life. This phenomenon has, *and is*, an unfathomable depth of love, light, peace and joy. The Light is all and is in all. That includes you and me and little children who die. Having remembered, I breathed deeply and relaxed. I recalled once again how exquisitely and perfectly life is set up even when it doesn't seem like it.

Reciting various names for the Divine during my prayers before I fall asleep is one way I remember Its true nature. (article #89) Reading the articles above and using the *Ask Your Soul, G.O.D. and Angels* technique are others.

### Q#2: Why would a loving God deceive us of our true identity and true home!

A#2: There's no deception by E.L.G.O.D. People / souls *choose* to forget who they are while visiting earth for reasons already discussed. Creator doesn't trick us. Beliefs to the contrary are the result of erroneous teachings and misinformation / lack of awareness about the nature of reality. We have to take responsibility for what we choose to focus on.

For example, how many people actively seek meaningful answers to life's biggest questions? In my experience, very few do until they are suffering or observing suffering. It's easier to watch idiotic game or 'reality' shows and keep tabs on which Hollywood stars are now dating.

Source wants all people to know who they are and that they can always be Home when they remember how life is set up. Our task is to learn who we are and what E.L.G.O.D. really is. How badly do we want to understand more about the greater reality? Struggles and suffering can be potent motivators to learn more about these important topics.

A wonderful story from India is instructive here. A student seeking to know more about The Divine asked a wise teacher for help. The teacher led the student into the river, pushed him under, and held him there despite his frantic struggles. When the student surfaced, he shouted: 'Why did you do that? I almost drowned!' The teacher replied, *'When you want to know God as much as you wanted a breath of air, you will see Her everywhere.'*

You likely came to earth, in part, to deepen your ability to *know and show*: (1) who you are, (2) why you are here, and (3) Who walks beside you.

It's one thing to know this and live accordingly when living in more sublime realms surrounded by your soulmates, guides, and angels. However, much greater lessons – and potentials for helping yourself and others – await those who can remember and demonstrate *'The Great News'* while suffering and seemingly separate from Source and loved ones.

**Once you really get this, it seems so simple**, but can admittedly be difficult to fully 'grok'. The following teachings helped me greatly during my journey of awakening…

- 'There is no spot where God is not'. – from *Christian Science* teachings
- 'There is only one power and one presence in the Universe and in my life – God, the Good Omnipotent'. – a *Unity* principle
- 'What you seek is seeking you'. – Rumi, Sufi poet and teacher
- Eternity does not start with death. We are in eternity now.' – Rev. Dr. Norman Vincent Peale, Christian minister
- 'Knowing that this body is like froth, knowing that its nature is that of a mirage, the disciple passes untouched by Death.' – Buddhism

- 'Deep within abides another life that escapes sight and is unchanging. The individual soul is nothing else in essence than universal soul.' – Hinduism

**Q#3: Why would a loving, caring, and powerful God allow such horrors as the holocaust and many other atrocities? I believe in God, have faith, and don't feel worthy to question Him. But so much suffering for so many innocent people? It breaks my heart.**

A#3: I recommend that you shift from the pronoun 'Him' to 'Her' or 'It' when referring to Source Energy. Just doing that makes many questions about seeming injustices seem ludicrous.
The movie *Oh God* (1977) can upgrade your understandings about The Divine and answer your question. God (played by George Burns) was asked by grocery store manager Jerry (played by John Denver):

> Jerry: *How can you permit all the suffering that goes on in the world?*
>
> God: *Ah, how can I permit the suffering? I don't permit the suffering. You do. Free will. All the choices are yours.*
>
> Jerry: *Choices? What choices?*
>
> God: *You can love each other, cherish and nurture each other or you can kill each other. You're also turning the sky into mud. I look down, I can't believe the filth. Using the rivers for toilets, poisoning my fishes.*

Polluting our air, water, and soil and excess use of chemicals is behind many common illnesses and deaths. How we treat our planet directly determines how much we, animals, and plants suffer. (#12, 37, 38)

Finally, you are eminently worthy of questioning The Above One because you are part and parcel of It. I understand how all the suffering can feel heart breaking. However, you can choose to reframe that: let it expand your heart and fuel your outreaches to grow, serve, and share your greatest gifts.

**Q#4: It seems that life is a pre-planned drama that includes so much trauma. Why would God cruelly set things up like this?**

A#4: Pre-planning is chosen by the souls / persons involved, not E.L.G.O.D. Ideally, people make these plans in conjunction with The Light and higher-energy assistance, but some do not. Once on earth, some people forget the big picture of life and ask the very question you did.

*Seeming* cruelty and drama have many benefits. For example, suffering is a potent way to awaken and more deeply remember the big picture of life. As I look back upon my time on earth, I can clearly see that the greatest growth was spurred by the deepest suffering. That has been well worth it in terms of improving my life and helping others.

And, too, remember that this earthly visit is very brief, relatively illusory, and only part of what our true selves are experiencing. The more you realize that, the more you can see drama and trauma as exquisite opportunities for more love, service, adventure, growth, and enjoyment.

**Q#5: I am all for earthly challenges, but taking my wife away from me is just pure evil. Why would He take her from me?**

A#5: It might seem like that to you, but no one took her away. Timing and meaning exists for when and how souls / people turn the page in Life's never-ending saga. Her bodily death – that seems to you to be untimely and cruel – may also have been a *pre-designed* way to awaken you in ways you wouldn't have otherwise. Understanding this important distinction can help you *have a breakthrough instead of a breakdown*.

# Question Section #17: Optimal Grieving

Grieving is a natural part of the human experience. It reflects the love and closeness you had with those who changed worlds. There is *a healthy range of mourning* that varies among individuals. During our radio interview, Dr. Wayne Dyer said that grief is shorter and less intense for self-actualized persons because they know death is not the end. I agree.

I have worked with people who still cry a lot every day ten years after a loved one passed on. Prolonged and severe grief can be a sign of physical and / or mental imbalances. Two examples of underlying causes are: (1) deficiencies of key nutrients for normal brain and endocrine functioning, and / or (2) multiple unresolved losses and traumas. Improved self-care and natural healing approaches addressing physical, mental, emotional, and spiritual needs can often help.

Excessive grieving serves no one. It ignores the facts of life after death and your eventual reunion. Severe and prolonged mourning also doesn't honor the person who graduated from earth school. Finally, being stuck in grief for a long time may block optimal communication with your postmaterial loved ones now.

**Articles**
*#3 When a Loved One's Earthly Body Dies*

*#8 When a Loved One's Earthly Form Is Dying*

*#9 Visiting 'Departed' Loved Ones Now*

*#22 When Your Pet Transitions from Earth*

*#62 I'll Still Be Sad...But Not As Much*

*#79 Changing Worlds in Just 8 Days*

*#82 Journey from 'Bereaved' to 'Shining Light'*

**Books:** *Radiant Wellness, Soul Proof, Greater Reality Living, The Eleven Questions*

**Audio Programs:** *Facilitated ADC; Holistic Breathing; The A.R.T. Technique; Ask Your Soul, G.O.D., and Angels*

**Q#1: My wife, who died due to a careless doctor, was / is compassionate and loved by many. It is very hard to live without her. She has come to me a few times full of light and love. I wasn't able to get any justice for her because of the underhandedness of the doctor. That has caused me much anger toward him and God. How am I supposed to carry on?**

A#1: Your anger is understandable. No one could blame you if you lived out your years in bitterness and discouragement.

However, your wife is now in a dimension where love, peace, joy, and other higher-energy emotions / ways of being predominate. *Her contacts that are full of light and love suggest that is true for her.* She isn't angry and hopeless about what happened. What appeared from a myopic earthly perspective to be a horrible injustice was her ticket back Home. People / souls move on in a timely manner even though it may appear to be premature and senseless to those with limited perspectives of the greater reality.

Even though it seems like it, you are not living without her. She is quite likely sending you love and visiting. You can continue a very real and wonderful relationship her now. In addition, *other parts of who you both really* are may be together now in another time and place.

That doesn't mean that you should condone or passively accept harm to others. If you feel called to do so, pursue legal means to ensure that the bodies of others aren't hurt or killed by this doctor. But take those actions with the intention of helping others, not out of anger and revenge. Your wife certainly doesn't need justice so don't do it for her. From her celestial vantage point, she can see the big picture and understands why things unfolded as they did.

Kudos for your accurate language: "My wife was / is a loving..." You are right since, except for her no-longer-needed earthly shell, SHE IS everything as before and much more. Remembering that can help you find and share the silver linings to this situation.

To assist your healing and positive transformation...

    1. *Let it be*: use the *Holistic Breathing Technique* to release anger, sadness, and other lower-energy emotions, and replace them with higher ones. (#25)

    2. Use the *Ask Your Soul, G.O.D. and Angels* technique to get in touch with your inner wisdom, understand why events unfolded as they did, and share the blessings.

    3. *Provide service to others* in her memory to upgrade your predominant emotions to joy, peace, and love. That will put you closer to the wavelength of her energy so you can better perceive your wife's presence now.

4. *Holistically care for yourself* as described in article #12 to tune-up your body / brain and release stress from the last few years.

You can be as angry at Creator and your higher-energy assistants for as long and as much as you want. They understand your pain and are assisting you now. Taking steps #1 – 4 above will help you sense and utilize their love, support, and guidance.

**Q#2: How can I get on the same vibrational level as my departed partner? Steve and I got into an argument just before he was hit by a car, and his family still blames me. They would not give me any of his ashes and are trying to gain custody of our children. I forgive his family for everything but feel like I can't heal as long as we are fighting.**

A#2: It *can seem* difficult to heal with all the lower-energy emotions involved: hatred, revenge, and bitterness from his family; guilt, hurt, and sadness for you. However, it is possible to move on. Follow my recommendations to A#1 above and:

    1. *Change yourself* and upgrade your perspective. As Gandhi taught: 'Be the change you wish to see in the world.' That will also make Steve very happy.

    2. *Realize it takes two or more to have a tug-of-war.* Let go of your end of the rope and feel the relief. This sets the stage for miracles to occur including healing between your family and his. I've seen and heard about this happening many times.

    3. *Remember that you can continue your relationship* with Steve. (article #9)

These steps will help you grieve fully so you and your children optimally grow and learn.

**Q#3: Our only child passed away last year, and now my husband has terminal cancer. I have to push down my grief for our son as I help my dying husband. How do I cope with all this? I feel as though I'm going to have a breakdown.**

A#3: It's very understandable that you feel like you might have a breakdown. Many people would under these circumstances. But there is another way to handle all this like the wise, infinite, and powerful being you are.

First, I hope you're not doing this alone or feel that you should. Have you 'called in the troops' and asked family and friends to help? Do you attend a supportive church / spiritual center where members – *some of whom may be 15%ers* – assist those in need? Have you contacted agencies in your area to help? That assistance will provide more time for rest, walking, eating healthfully, processing, and relaxing so you don't become ill or imbalanced.

Use my recommendations under A#1. Use Nutritional Response Testing or Applied Kinesiology and other natural healing approaches discussed in article #12 to help you avoid a nervous breakdown. Be sure to set aside quality time for you and your husband.

Your husband might benefit from hearing and seeing your grief instead of you pushing it down. You two raised your son together; now you can grieve together and help each other. Your husband might *welcome the opportunity* to grieve openly before he crosses over. It's so difficult for many men to mourn the bodily death of a child. He doesn't need to carry lower-energy emotions into his next phase of life.

In addition to the above, read article #8 and listen to the *Radio Shows* on SoulProof.com. After your husband has transitioned, you may need to 'collapse' for a while and really focus on healing and resting. As your energy and balance increase, you can turn your attention to gaining a greater reality perspective that helps all this make more sense. Then you can begin to identify, benefit from, and share the silver linings that always accompany tough challenges.

# QUESTION SECTION #18: WHEN A CHILD CHANGES WORLDS

*If death is an illusion, the death of a child is the cruelest of all illusions.* This sentence speaks volumes about how difficult it can be when a child of any age passes on by any means. No parents ever want to bury their children and, yet, it happens so often. I have been honored to help many bereaved parents and family members, especially during the last eight years through *Helping Parents Heal*.

When visiting with my grandchildren, I sometimes call them *you so-called children*. Around age ten, one asked why I call them that. That provided a perfect teaching moment for reminding them and me that, **even though they look / act / and talk like a child, they are really much more than that.** We read *The Big Picture of Life* book together and discussed their questions and fears about life, death, and afterlife.

*That distinction – looking like immature and helpless children, but actually being timeless and powerful beings of energy / consciousness – is of paramount importance.* Really knowing that can help you find meaning, peace, and blessings when a child changes worlds.

## Articles
*#2 When a Child Changes Worlds*

*#4 When a Loved One Passes On by Suicide*

*#9 Visiting 'Departed' Loved Ones Now*

*#25 Pre-Birth Planning: Did I REALLY Choose All This?*

*#41 The A.R.T. Technique*

*#82 Journey from 'Bereaved' to 'Shining Light'*

*#93 For Bereaved Parents and Family Members*

**Books:** *The Big Picture of Life, Soul Proof, Greater Reality Living, The Eleven Questions*

**Audio Programs:** *Heal and Transform Your Suffering; Pre-Birth Planning; Holistic Breathing; Facilitated After Death Contact; Ask Your Soul, G. O.D., and Angels*

**Q#1: Two weeks ago, a distracted driver ran into my daughter's car and she was killed. Her two children were hurt and live with me now. I am desperately trying to "feel" my baby and know she's OK, but I just feel cold instead. I pray, but feel only sadness.**

A#1: Two weeks is not very long so it's very common to feel that way. Not feeling your daughter is probably due to you being in so much pain and shock. She may be trying to get through to you, but you understandably can't receive her transmissions. Be assured that she is being attended to by angels, guides, and The One. You might be able to sense her later but, for now, you need to focus on yourself and the little ones. I recommend the following:

    1. Read the articles listed above and take relevant action steps.

2. Contact *Helping Parents Heal* and attend online and in-person meetings. Use their *Caring Listeners*, a group of amazing parents that I started and provide clinical support for.

3. Reach out to family, friends, church members, and social agencies. You don't have to go through this alone.

You are beginning a long journey that will be difficult at times, but *you can make it by taking one day at a time.* Your life won't be the same as it was before your daughter's passing. But you can eventually experience more love, joy, peace, and meaning than you can imagine. First steps? Hold that vision and follow my recommendations and those of your support team.

**Q#2: My youngest son recently changed worlds. (Thank you for that term.) He was the first in our family to transition besides distant relatives. I don't know who he's with or who met him when he transitioned. This, along with so many other racing thoughts, leaves me paralyzed with grief at times.**

A#2: What mother wouldn't worry that he might be alone? *However, nothing could be further from the truth.* He is literally surrounded – as are you and everyone else – by many dear ones. These include soulmates he has known for eons but weren't on earth this time around the wheel. He is also lovingly ministered to by his angels, guides, master teachers, and – always and everywhere – The Light.

Your son can, or soon will be able to, visit loved ones still on earth. That may be especially true during family gatherings and holidays when you need it the most. He is very likely having a wonderful time. If you could hear him right now, he would tell you that **no one is ever really alone here or in the hereafter.** Since he crossed over at a young age, he is likely an advanced soul who has been through the process of birth and death many times. Please don't worry about him; instead, attend to yourself and your family.

As for your other racing thoughts, those are common and can be addressed. Use the resources listed under #A1, especially the *Caring Listeners* who have been through the worst and are now shining light parents. They will listen to anything you want to talk about, share what worked for them, and suggest resources. If your racing thoughts persist, I suggest nutrition-based healing as discussed in article #12 to make sure your brain and adrenal glands are functioning normally.

**Q#3: You say children who die young are often more highly evolved souls. Since I have lost two children and am now 87, I must be a very young soul. I am being a bit facetious. But beneath that is a tremendous amount of pain, anger, disappointment, and disbelief in a loving and all powerful God.**

A#3: Bravo for stating so well what many people feel. I'm glad you were being a bit facetious. You may be an evolved being who agreed to have two children pass on and demonstrate that you can keep going. You may have volunteered to stick around to serve and teach others. Please read the articles above to learn more about these possibilities.

You are entitled to feel pain, anger, and more as long and as much as you want. However, given the quality of your note and words, I suspect you aren't the kind to stay in a rut. Reaching out to me suggests that you are ready to reach higher ground. You can feel happier and more peaceful again. I hope this book helps you do that.

As for your disbelief in a Higher Power, join the club. I and many people have wrestled with that very question after seeing and / or experiencing deep loss. I went through a transition FROM seeing

'God' as a huge protective father (all powerful, loving, and knowing) TO my current views. Given what you've been through, you may want to review Question Section #2 to internalize more contemporary and sensible images of Source.

The Creator and Sustainer of All Life certainly understands your doubt and anger. Talk with Her about it daily until you remember that life is an oft changing but never-ending dance of love, light, and energy.

**Q#4: My son transitioned 7 months ago. I am going through a transformation and now see the world differently than before. I've experienced numerous contacts from him, so I totally know he still exists in another dimension. He was only 13 years old, but I believe his soul was much older than that. I agree there is a rhyme and reason behind the timing of his transition, but sometimes fall back into old patterns of thinking. I occasionally blame myself and wonder if I could have done anything to prevent his departure. That is in conflict with the belief that we had an agreement about this. What is your advice?**

A#4: It's *a question of balance*, isn't it? Where is the emotional heart if you callously say, 'Oh well, it was preplanned.' On the other hand, being stuck in a self-defeating loop of 'What if?' doesn't honor how magnificently life is set up. Sit with those feelings and, at the same time, remember that meaning and timing exist as life unfolds. That stance will help you heal, remain awakened, and live fully in this world.

It's natural to sometimes fall back into old patterns of thinking that your son's passing was a random tragedy that wouldn't have occurred if only you had (fill in the blank). Feeling guilt and self-blame is nearly universal for bereaved parents. The trick is to catch lower-energy thoughts as soon as possible, remember the big picture of life, and replace them with higher ones. With this approach, you can increasingly become a shining light parent.

Read and re-read the articles listed for this section, especially #25 about the possibility of pre-birth planning. Just knowing *there may be* a greater meaning and timing behind tragedy can lighten your grieving. Take time to pray, do yoga, meditate, and walk in nature. Over time, all this can help transmute conflict into remembering. You can develop an inner knowing and peace that will bless others and yourself. You can be sure that your son – who is likely one of your teachers – will be smiling brightly as he sees that your plan is working.

**Q#5: My youngest child died recently. I am trying everything to lessen this searing pain and deep longing to be with my boy. I am not suicidal; I just don't want to live in this world without him. This make me feel guilty because I truly love my older children.**

A#5: I've heard numerous parents say the same thing, so you aren't alone in that respect. My sense is that, although you love all your children, there was and is a special connection with your son who graduated from earth-school. It sounds like more than him being 'the baby' of the family. There's no need to feel guilty; many parents have a favorite whether they like to admit it or not.

Regarding losing your will to live, that is also quite common in early to middle stages of grieving. Good parents want to ensure their child is safe and happy, even when the child is living in a nonearthly realm. And, as you say, the pain and sadness are so severe. It's very understandable that parents sometimes feel like they can't handle it anymore.

Please read the articles mentioned above and take relevant action steps to begin healing and transforming. Over time, you can find a way to be peaceful and joyful again. That will serve you, your family members, and everyone you meet.

# Question Section #19: When a Loved One Passes On

(Note: This section applies to persons who aren't children.) As you know, a vast amount of clinical and scientific evidence clearly shows that life continues after bodily death. In addition, many firsthand experiences show that life does not end when the earthly body perishes. This collective evidence sets the stage for *optimally responding* when a loved one changes worlds.

Everyone is unique so what you need to best handle this change can vary. The more pieces you find to this apparent puzzle, the more you can understand the big picture. Many resources and teachers are there to help you during this time of need. In addition, many role models have demonstrated other ways to react besides suffering and deep grief. Given all this, you don't have to automatically feel prolonged and intense pain, sadness, and loneliness anymore. There are higher-energy ways to respond given what we now know.

**Articles**
#3 When a Loved One's Earthly Body Dies

#25 Pre-Birth Planning: Did I REALLY Choose All This?

#41 The A.R.T. Technique

#62 I'll Still Be Sad... But Not As Much

*#82 Journey from 'Bereaved' to 'Shining Light'*

**Books:** *Soul Proof, The Eleven Questions, The Afterlife Evidence, Greater Reality Living*

**Audio Programs:** *Facilitated After Death Contact; Holistic Breathing; Pre-Birth Planning; Ask Your Soul, G.O.D. and Angels*

**Q#1: My husband passed away recently after a long and debilitating illness. I feel completely devoid of everything, just an echoing emptiness where there was once life and love. I am lost without him. I know there is no help, nor do I expect any. No questions, just thank you for reading.**

A#1: I understand, at least in part, how you feel. But, actually, there is help available. As the old saying goes, "I'm too busy to fall apart now. I'll do it after the crisis is over." Your job of helping him transition from earth is over. Now you're feeling the predictable crash of it all plus grief and emptiness.

You're not the first and won't be the last to feel this way. Healing and transforming depend upon your openness to that, and action steps you take. We each co-create our own realities. Yours will be bleak and hopeless if you keep making such dire statements and believing there is no hope. I'm not being critical, just reminding you that 'As you think, so shall you be.' You didn't mention if have a history of loss and / or depression but it sounds likely.

My recommendations for you ...

    1. Read the articles listed above and make graduated changes. You may have to push yourself at first since his passing is recent and you feel so devastated.

2. Read articles #12, 26, and 32 to learn about holistic health, especially nutrition-based healing from a practitioner who uses Nutrition Response Testing or Applied Kinesiology. They can help you balance your brain, adrenal glands, thyroid, and other organs that may have become fatigued or exhausted.

3. Take time to be good to yourself. Get extra rest, curl up and enjoy a cup of tea, read good books, enjoy great movies, and take walks in nature.

4. Reach out to family, friends, and others who can help. Given your words, I suspect it's difficult for you to ask for help but I hope you do. Don't isolate yourself.

5. Use the *Ask Your Soul, G.O.D. and Angels* technique to access wisdom and guidance about how to optimally move forward in all aspects of your life.

6. When you feel ready, see article #9 to facilitate your awareness of his living presence. Your relationship was so close that sensing him may be fairly easy after some R & R.

**Q#2: I found my one true soulmate, but she died just when we were about to start a new chapter in our life together. Before then, I had been selfish and a hypocrite. Was her death a punishment for my wrong deeds?**

A#2: I am sorry for your suffering but glad you are seeking to understand how to move forward optimally. Part of your suffering is due to guilt, self-blame, and beliefs based on past erroneous teachings. More accurate and contemporary evidence indicate that:

1. You have a few dozen primary and many more secondary soulmates, not just one. I'm not minimizing your pain but that wasn't

your only shot at having a very happy and deeply connected relationship. We get more than one chance at real love.

2. Life and Creator DO NOT punish us. We punish ourselves by:

a. believing ignorant and fear-based teachings

b. creating ripples / karma from past lower-energy thoughts, words, and deeds

c. not listening to our inner guidance and wise counsel from others.

d. getting stuck in grief versus searching for blessings and new beginnings.

You can punish yourself for your lower-energy actions, but that just creates more of the same. Your sadness can be a potent wake-up call and blessing in disguise. Before coming to earth, you may have designed the possibility of this outcome because of your habit of being selfish and thoughtless toward others. She may have volunteered, out of love, to help you remember and do better. You two may be dear soulmates who created this plan for important reasons. Will you remember the big picture and create meaning from it?

From a limited earthly perspective, yours was a tragic and unfair event that could cause you to suffer long and hard. However, from a greater reality perspective, it an excellent opportunity designed to learn, grow, and help others. I hope you choose the latter option. Use the resources listed above to find meaning and enjoy the benefits.

***Q#3: Your articles resonate very deeply with me. I have had three sudden deaths to cope with: my three-year-old sister died in a car accident when I was 16; my father died when I was 19; and my brother passed away recently. My brother's death was on the same month and day that my father died. Is there a connection between their deaths? I am trying so hard to appreciate all I have and not live in fear. But I am struggling.***

A#3: Perhaps your dad and brother graduating from earth school on the same date is *a way of making you look at life more deeply.* Their transitioning from earth on the same date got your attention, didn't it? It may have been *a prearranged signal* to motivate you to ask important questions and find sensible answers. Many people don't do this until they are suffering or dying – and some not even then. Head-scratching events can shake up your world and make you ask, "What in the world is going on?"

Bravo for intending to appreciate what you have and not live in fear. Those are two big keys to creating an optimal earthly experience. **As for struggling, the importance of that isn't sufficiently appreciated.** Have you every lifted weights and strained to get that last rep in? Struggling, even though you feel like quitting, can make a big difference in muscle growth. Developing a greater strength of spirit is very similar. Adversity can help you reach down deep and discover who you really are.

The resulting higher consciousness and inner strength becomes – **great news alert here** – a continuing part of who you are now AND in the future. To the awakening mind, that is easily worth the effort and temporary pain. Your sister, brother, and dad may have volunteered, out of love, to help you with this lesson. *Life is inviting you* to realize just how safe, meaningful, and magnificent this brief earthly experience is. How will you respond?

# Question Section #20: When a Loved One's Body Dies by Suicide

My interest in suicide prevention began while working in hospitals and trying to resuscitate young people who took pills or shot themselves. I provided suicide counseling and education while in theology school and have continued that with many people over the last 45 years. Death is tough enough on loved ones when it happens by illness, injury, murder, or natural causes. It's even worse with suicide since people decide to kill their bodies or, at least, increase that probability by drug addiction, drunk driving, and other irresponsible behaviors.

The Centers for Disease Control and Prevention state that the U.S. suicide rate increased 33% from 2009 to 2019. It's now the second most common cause of death for ages 10 – 34. I consider suicide to be an epidemic for which holistic solutions are severely needed. Those who pass on by suicide are in pain, imbalanced, overwhelmed, and / or feel like they just can't handle life on earth any longer. I discuss common causes of suicide in my book *Radiant Wellness*.

I've worked with many people whose loved ones passed on by suicide. The initial shock is often followed by profound guilt and self-blame. The thought *'What if I would have done more to help?'* repeats over and over until the body, especially brain and hormonal organs, become exhausted. Loved ones 'left behind' on earth often feel anger that the suicidal person didn't try or reach out for help more. Then they sometimes feel even more guilty about those thoughts and further beat themselves up. Archaic, fear-based religious teachings about suicide being a one-way ticket to eternal hell make all this even more scary and painful.

Given the devastating impact of suicide, conscious language is crucial. That's why the title of this section is carefully worded: **your loved one didn't die by suicide, just his / her earthly body did.** *That distinction is so important.* Just focusing on that difference has helped some people start to heal. Please post it where you will see it often so you can upgrade your beliefs, thoughts, and words about what happened.

## Articles
*#3 When a Loved One's Earthly Body Dies*

*#4 When a Loved One Passes On by Suicide*

*#6 Evidential Mediums*

*#9 Visiting 'Departed' Loved Ones Now*

*#36 Suicide: Core Causes and Holistic Solutions*

**Books:** *Soul Proof, Greater Reality Living, Radiant Wellness*

**Audio Programs:** *Holistic Breathing Technique; Heal and Transform Your Suffering; Pre-Birth Planning; Love, Acceptance, and Forgiveness Technique; Facilitated ADC*

**Q#1: My husband ended his earthly life recently. It is the most horrific experience I have ever gone through. I miss him terribly, and still think there must have been something I could have said or done to help him. Any help would be so deeply appreciated.**

A#1: I am impressed that you are seeking sensible solutions so soon. Kudos for your conscious language of 'ended his earthly life' instead of 'he killed himself.' If a person has serious suicidal intention, family and friends can't really say or do anything that will make a difference. If put in an in-patient unit, they will try again when they get out. Feeling guilt and responsibility are common but unfortunate responses to a very tough situation. I recommend the following to begin healing:

1. **Remember that suicide is NOT the end of life or a one-way ticket to 'hell.'** Suicide is a ticket back Home for those who, for whatever reason, can no longer tolerate this earthly experience. Categories of clinical evidence that indicate this is so include near death experiences, evidential medium readings, Life Between Lives(R) sessions, and after death communications.

2. Read article #4 and take action steps

3. Listen to 'Ask the Soul Doctors' *Radio Shows* in which I and other experts answer the question, "What happens to those who transition by suicide?"

4. Read the 'Suicide: NOT An Unforgivable Sin' section in my book *Soul Proof*. This will help you know that suicide is not a certain ticket to fire and brimstone forever.

5. Use the first four audio programs *in the order listed above* to heal and transform.

6. Have an evidential medium session so you know he really is alive and well. (article #6)

7. When you are ready to continue a different but highly meaningful relationship with him, read article #9 and use the *Facilitated ADC* technique.

All of this won't totally remove your pain and sadness over night, but it should lighten the intensity and duration of it. Later, you may feel called to serve others in his honor; that will help them and assist your healing. After all, those are common reasons why people / souls volunteer to possibly go through such pain: remember their true nature, grow, serve, and expand love and peace in themselves and our world.

**Q#2: My best friend lost his job, apartment, and girlfriend. He shot himself in the head after promising me he would never do that. He was an intelligent guy with a college degree. His parents were dead, and he lived alone. I am feeling so many tough emotions and don't know how to move forward.**

A#2: That is a difficult one, especially given the violent method of suicide and his promise to you. You tried to help so his decision could understandably cause:

1. guilt that you didn't intervene more and / or differently

2. anger that he put you in this situation

3. hopelessness about not being able to do more about it

4. concern about him if you believe suicide causes lasting spiritual damage or torment

5. being confronted with your own discouragement and fear of death

*The list of negative repercussions can go on and on, but it doesn't have to.* See my list of recommendations under A#1 and take action steps. Over time, many people have realized that their loved ones who transitioned by suicide are – or soon will be – happy, peaceful, and living fully in the here and now moment. And they want you to feel the same way.

Why do I say 'are or soon will be'? Depending on a number of factors, those who pass on via suicide may feel remorse about their actions, guilt about pain caused to loved ones, and sadness about missing others. This may especially be true when, for example, a young person impulsively chooses suicide after a first love break or while under the influence of alcohol and / or drugs. However, those are self-induced and temporary feelings, not eternal states meted out by a judgmental 'God'. The postmaterial person can feel better and resume the flow of life as they forgive themselves, learn lessons, and vow to do better in the future.

**Q#3: My teenage daughter passed on by suicide three years ago. Your articles and books kept me from dropping into a deep depression. Why are so many children choosing suicide?**

A#3: Thank you for asking this very important question. At that age, they ought to be thinking about sports, romance, friends, pets, comic books, and other fun topics. Young people who choose suicide are like canaries in a coalmine warning the rest of us about what we have done to our air, food, water, and nature. **What will it take for a sufficient number of people to awaken to this and do something about it?** It starts with you and me.

My answers to your question are more fully addressed in article #36. For example, the brains of young people have been flooded with unnatural and harmful factors such as...

1. Pesticides and herbicides sprayed on foods that aren't organic.

2. Excess vaccinations: many are now medically recommended *by school age.*

3. Pharmaceutical drugs, especially pain killers, prescribed when safe and natural methods can often address the underlying problems.

4. Junk food, sugar, artificial sweeteners, and chemical additives that act as neuro-stimulants and neuro-toxins.

5. Wheat that absorbs many times more pesticides and herbicides than other grains. (Even organic wheat can cause GI and brain-focus issues for some people.)

6. Plastic particles and other chemicals that prevent normal functioning of the brain and endocrine organs.

7. Deficiency of key nutrients. (Most young people don't get those even if they eat a healthy diet. Why? Unless it's organic, most foods are raised in topsoil depleted of vitamins, minerals, and co-nutrients.)

8. Lack of parental supervision and guidance due to one-parent families, both parents working, and / or overly permissive child raising approaches.

9. Excessive exposure to mentally over-stimulating TV shows, video games, porn, etc.

10. Not having sensible spiritual teachings and exposure to kindred spirits.

11. Lack of basic self-care practices such as sufficient rest, sunshine, activity, and healthy leisure activities involving family and friends.

This holistic approach is needed to get to the root causes of the growing suicide epidemic in younger people. It's easy to blame Big Pharma, Big Agra, Big Oil, Big Insurance, and Big Disease Care industries for #1 – 7 since their profit-orientations hurt and kill so many people and our planet. **But complaining won't fix the problem. We each need to take responsibility and demand healthier products even if they cost more.** Businesses will produce safer and healthier products when enough people demand that and are willing to pay for it.

Do you think you don't have the time, energy, and / or money to address those eleven criteria? In the long run, *you will save all three* by avoiding predictable health problems, treatment costs, and tragedies. Please share this information with others so that children can grow up without what Mark Hyman MD calls 'broken brains'.

**Q#4: My son ended his life last year. I went to church and was told that those who die by suicide go to hell. My preacher said he made his choice to die that way and must pay for it. He inferred that my son couldn't be with God. Those comments made me wonder what kind of God would act that way. After visiting your website and getting signs from my son, I have more hope.**

A#4: I look forward to the day when preachers quit spewing horribly archaic and ignorant information about a loving Creator. I say 'preachers' because most ministers who earn Bachelor and

Master of Divinity (M.Div.) degrees wouldn't teach such fear-based drivel. Have you considered finding a different church that focuses on – as Jesus taught – peace, love, unity, forgiveness, letting your light shine, and service to others?

Over the years, I've received many similar notes from bereaved parents whose churches failed them during their darkest hour. When suicide is involved, some ministers don't know what to say. When a child passes on other ways, ministers say :'It was God's will' or 'God works in mysterious ways' – as if either of those help at all. A bizarre and cruel response is: 'God wanted to be with your little one'. Is that supposed to comfort the parents and fill them with confidence about such a Creator who works that way?

Some ministers were well-meaning and just passed on what they had been taught. Others probably felt inadequate and repeated some trite comment. My pastoral counseling training certainly didn't address what to say in such situations. Most ministers don't know the collective evidence behind *'The Great News'* listed in the *Introduction*.

Congratulations for listening to your heart and trusting how a loving and fair Creator would act. Your reward will be discovering sensible answers that benefit you and others. As a youth, I struggled with fundamentalist teachings that focused much more on fear and hell than love and heaven. In the years since, I've found many loving, wise, open-minded, and open-hearted places of worship. See A#5 under Question Section #9 to see that list.

PS – With much love and respect, I suggest using more conscious language than 'My son ended his life.' **He didn't end his life, just this earthly experience. The difference between the two is vast.** Saying 'my son ended this earthly experience' sounds more cumbersome, but it's much more accurate and comforting.

**Q#5: My husband took his own life 24 years ago. He was a wonderful person but was very depressed. Since those who pass on by suicide enter a different realm than those passing on naturally, are they ever able to achieve higher realms? Or is it their destiny to always be separated from their loved ones?**

A#5: Lots of statements are made, without supportive evidence, about the afterlife. Think about it from the perspective of a good parent. What if (1) your child was very depressed and / or otherwise imbalanced and in pain, and (2) she made a decision that she wouldn't consider if not for factor #1. Would you say to her, "You think you had it bad? I'll show you what bad really is! You will be separated from your loved ones forever!"

Would even an average earthly parent do that? Of course not. How, then, can anyone believe that the Creator and Sustainer of All Life could even imagine this uncaring and punitive response?

I wouldn't say that those who transition by suicide necessarily enter a different realm. They may or may not – depending on a number of factors – need more rest, recharging, and counseling compared to those who cross over by natural means. If more intensive care is needed, he can rejoin his soul group afterwards and reenter the stream of life.

Your husband will not be separated from his loved ones forever. That might be how ignorant and uncaring people would handle it, but not The Ground of All Being.

**Q#6: I have worried about my wife's soul since she died by suicide. I'm afraid she will be punished for that. Will God ever forgive her so she can reach higher realms?**

A#6: Oh my, no wonder life on earth is so difficult. There are enough real problems without needlessly fearing a vengeful 'God' who condemns, punishes, and might not forgive. Suicide is such a big decision that isn't taken lightly. There's no external punishment, especially for someone who obviously suffered before resorting to suicide in an attempt to find some peace.

*She might judge and punish herself for a while* much like we do on earth after making lower-energy choices. Over time, however, she can heal and improve just like we can here.

The reasons for suicide vary greatly. Hers might have been a possibility discussed during pre-birth planning. Why? To help awaken others about what we are doing to our planet and the negative repercussions for people, animals, and plants. For example, if she suffered with cancer or mental illness, her action might motivate more people to improve conditions and prevent worse problems in the future.

*A Course in Miracles* teaches that Creator doesn't forgive because She never condemned in the first place. Also remember that your wife is an integral part of All That Is right now and always. So why would G.O.D. need to forgive Itself? Higher realms are always available – for her and all of us – when we awaken to our true natures and live accordingly. That is always possible no matter what we have done in the past, including suicide.

# Question Section #21: When a Pet Transitions to Next Phase of Life

Some people feel closer to and receive more love from pets than from people. They feel that these 'furry spirits' embody unconditional love and acceptance. Many animals are loyal, loving, and grateful – qualities sometimes lacking in humans. It's not surprising that many people grieve deeply when a beloved animal moves back into The Field of All Possibilities.

The stages of grief can be similar to those when beloved persons graduate from earth-school. You may experience denial, anger, bargaining, and depression before accepting that your dear pet has changed worlds. Your sadness may be triggered by a memory or finding a play toy while cleaning. Nearly every day, I'm asked: 'Is my cat still alive and happy in another place?", 'Does my dog still remember and love me?', and the most common one *'Will I see my beloved pet again?'* **The short answers are yes, yes, and yes.**

## Articles
*#22 When Your Pet Transitions from Earth*

*#39 In Honor of Lila the Cat*

# When a Pet Transitions to Next Phase of Life

*#81 A Dove's Message*

**Books:** *Soul Proof, Greater Reality Living*

**Audio Programs:** *Facilitated After Death Contact; A.R.T.; Ask Your Soul, G.O.D., and Angels*

### Q#1: Do animals have an afterlife?

A#1: Multiple categories of evidence indicate that, as with people, the life force / energy of animals continues living after bodily death:

    a. *Evidential mediums* often report seeing pets and may provide specific details such as name, color, and mode of bodily death. Some of these sessions occur under controlled conditions so mediums could not have collected this information before the reading. (article #6)

    b. *After death communications* (ADCs) are another way that many people have perceived their postmaterial pets. Many people have reported seeing, hearing, and feeling the presence of their furry spirits. (article #28)

    c. *Death bed visions* are a third category of evidence that points to the continued existence of pets after bodily death. Some people who are near death describe seeing postmaterial pets who assist the dying person to return Home. Astonishingly, some doctors, nurses, and visiting family members sometimes also see these postmaterial escorts. A scene at 31:00 in the movie *Talking to Heaven* wonderfully depicts this. (article #95)

    d. *Near death experiences* are well recognized after decades of investigation by esteemed physicians, psychologists, and university professors. After nearly dying, some people return to describe being greeted by pets who passed on previously. (article #94)

### Q#2: My beloved dog Rex died recently. Will I see him again?

A#2: The energy in all life – whether in humans, animals, plants, etc. – is indestructible. The outward appearance changes form but the inherent energy still exists. After bodily death, that energy can manifest in a different time / space variation. From a more spiritual / religious perspective, their love and spirit continue and can appear in new ways.

The clinical evidence reviewed in A#1 indicates that you will see Rex again. He can appear to you in whatever way will be most comforting and recognizable. That could be in a physical canine form, or as multi-colored light/energy that you know is him. Either way, you can have a glorious reunion when you change worlds. You may not have to wait until you change worlds to encounter him again. Rex may come back to you as a different pet during this earthly experience. (Some people have noticed significant similarities between a new and postmaterial pet. Dreams and psychic readings sometimes precede these possible pet reunions.) You also can visit during a *Facilitated ADC* session (article #9)

### Q#3: I know my beloved pets live on, but will they join me in the afterlife?

A#3: As #5 in *'The Great News'* reminds us, all life is sacredly interconnected. That is especially so for those who have enjoyed very close relationships. The powers of love and intention are so strong that they can shape reality. If having a reunion is your and their vision, it likely will happen. In addition, as with people, the

## When a Pet Transitions to Next Phase of Life

consciousness of animals may be able to embody in more than one place at the same time. As such, you and your pets may be together right now in another slice of life.

**Q#4: Two weeks ago, I lost Ivy, my beloved pet of 18 years. My grief is as bad as anything I have experienced in my life. I feel that part of my energy went with her. In some sense, might we still be together and connected?**

A#4: I am glad that you two had so many great years together and created such wonderful memories. Part of your energy may have gone with her for a while. Some people do that to ensure that their loved ones get settled into their new abode. It's not really needed, but it is understandable among those who are very close.

Two weeks isn't very long so of course you are deeply grieving. However, if that grief continues to be severe over time, you might want to handle it a different way. Shamans and Native American healers recognize that *part of soul's energy can get stuck or separated from the core*. Medical mediums like Caroline Myss describe a person's energetic circuit breakers turning off.

This may be adaptive for a while as the person gets over the shock and sadness. Over time, though, stuck energy could contribute to physical and / or mental symptoms. That also may prevent you from sensing Ivy and other 'departed' loved ones from your earthly vantage point. I recommend *Holistic Breathing* and the *Heal and Transform Your Suffering* technique (articles #70 and 84) to release pain and reconnect with your body.

Finally, conscious language makes such a difference when a loved one changes worlds. Say the following two phrases aloud and notice which one feels more accurate and comforting: 'I lost Ivy' versus 'Ivy transitioned to the next phase of life'.

**Q#5: My beloved cat Princess died last week. We were very close for many years. Do you think she is still aware of me?**

A#5: Given how close you were, it's very likely that she is still aware of you. Your deep heart-to-heart connection continues despite the death of her earthly form. Because of their loving energy, pets naturally gravitate to beatific realms in the afterlife. You'll want to fine tune your thoughts, words, and deeds so you are on a similar wavelength. One way to sense Princess now is to live with peace, joy, love, and other higher energies / ways of being. (article #100)

That includes taking the high road in your grieving about her. Rather than becoming enmired in sadness as some people do, you can choose – moment by moment – to focus on Appreciation for all the great times, memories, and love. You can Realize your eternal connection and Transform yourself for the better. To learn about the A.R.T. technique, see article #41.

**Q#6: I lost my pregnant pet cat Susie yesterday and am feeling extremely guilty and sad about not caring for her better. She was very close to my heart, but I failed to notice her anemic condition. I am very busy as a single working woman and have 12 other rescued cats and 3 dogs at home. I also feed about 25 street dogs every night after I return from my job.**

A#6: I hope you know that you can never really lose people or pets with whom you have strong heart connections. Remembering that should help the sadness you feel. There's also no need for guilt Susie is enjoying a place of peace, love, and happiness right now – and wants you to do the same. Her consciousness understood that you have so many animals you are helping. She was fine with that, and it was her time to move on.

This also might be a sign that it's time to be more balanced and take care of yourself. Pat yourself on the back for all you do and release the guilt.

# Question Section #22: When a Loved One's Physical Form is Murdered

A loved one's earthly form being murdered could understandably haunt and hobble you for the rest of your days on earth. Anger, hatred, bitterness, and desire for revenge could become the central focus in your life.

*Or the murder could trigger a spiritually transformative experience that results in amazing benefits for you and others.*

Because those lower-energy emotions *feel* so intense, some people aren't aware that **a choice exists.** Society reinforces how terrible you should feel when certain events such as murder and suicide occur. But *there's an intermediate step between the event and how you feel.* You can choose to pause and remember the big picture of life before reacting. (article #91)

I'm not judging those who, after the murder of a loved one's form, don't make higher-energy choices. However, it is possible to look for blessings and ways to honor your loved one. Taking the high road doesn't condone murder or advocate a lack of legal punishment. But it does recognize there is *a great way* in life than many people cannot fathom. This middle road recognizes that things are not always as they seem. As such, we cannot see the big picture of life, especially when horrific events occur.

Consider the poem *Brahma* by Ralph Waldo Emerson that recognizes the timeless and deathless nature of people: *"If the slayer thinks he slays, or if the slain thinks he is slain, they know not well the subtle ways I keep, and pass, and turn again."*

Here's another way to look at it. There are only five ways a non-elderly person can change worlds when it's time: illness, accident, unknown causes, suicide, and murder. From a limited earthly perspective, all of these seem horrible. However, from a greater reality viewpoint, all of them are a ticket to the next phase of life. How else can a soul in a younger person's body graduate except by what appears to be an extremely sad and bad event?

## Articles
*#3 When a Loved One's Earthly Body Dies*

*#27 When a Loved One's Earthly Body Is Murdered…*

**Books:** *Soul Proof, The Big Picture of Life*

**Audio Programs:** *Holistic Breathing; Heal and Transform Your Suffering; Love, Acceptance, and Forgiveness; Facilitated After Death Contact*

**Q#1: My boyfriend was murdered five weeks ago, and I was there. I was raised in church and don't want God to punish me for questioning, but I just want to know if he is OK. How does someone so traumatized like me find comfort?**

A#1: You can be assured that he is much more than OK. Depending on the circumstances before his murder, he may require deep rest, healing, and reorientation before rejoining his team. Then he can begin learning from his experience, growing, and continuing his journey through forever. Depending on several factors, he may be able to contact you sooner or later in that process.

It's very difficult to find comfort this soon after seeing the body of your loved one murdered. (*Your boyfriend wasn't actually murdered, remember? His earthly body was* and that is less than 1% of who and what he really is.) The key for you now is survival: take one day at a time, rest, recharge, and heal. Pray for and visualize a healing shower from your angels, guides, and the Light. Let others help you and lean on them. Later, you can pay it forward.

Read the articles above and take recommended action steps. When you feel ready, use the audio programs in the order they are listed. That will help you to, respectively:

1. release anger, deep grief and other lower-energy emotions

2. heal and transform even after this

3. begin the process of loving, accepting, and forgiving whomever you need to

4. develop a different but meaningful way of interacting with him

You don't have to worry about The Divine punishing you for questioning. It's also common to feel very angry at Creator and life after a trauma like that. The Infinite One understands all the difficult emotions you are going through and doesn't take questioning and anger personally. If your church teaches that 'God' punishes those who question, I would find a different spiritual center with more evolved teachings and people. (article #16)

## When a Loved One's Physical Form is Murdered

**Q#2: My parents were murdered 12 years ago, but I haven't had any signs from them. How can I know if they are doing OK?**

A#2: Here's the good news... even though you haven't perceived contact from your parents, you can be sure they are alive and well in the next phase of life. Their consciousness that energized their 'parent disguises' didn't disappear or cease to exist. That life force is now manifesting in a different way but your daughter – parent connection continues to be sacred, important, and very real.

They are likely actively trying to get hold of you so you may want to work on being more receptive. An exception might be if there is *a prearranged plan to the contrary*. For example, they may withhold signs so you can search and deepen your knowing that life and love do not die. Struggling about this for a while can build 'spiritual muscles' that serve you and others here and in the hereafter. Using the audio programs listed above will likely increase your direct perception of them.

**Q#3: Just 6 months ago, my poor boy was stabbed in the heart and died soon after. I'm feeling so numb and lost. He was begging for an ambulance before he died. Do you think he suffered much?**

A#3: Six months is very recent, so of course you are feeling numb and lost. *It can feel horrible when you can't see his outer shell.* You didn't really 'lose' your son, but it certainly seems like it. That's why you need to remember and focus on the other 99% of who and what he is.

To begin the journey of healing, start by reading articles and using resources listed in Question Section #18 for bereaved parents. Information, action steps, support, and time can help you move past the shock, despair, and pain.

Many parents would wonder, and even obsess, about whether and how much their child suffered. Good evidence indicates that *the consciousness of a person can disengage from the body just before a fatal injury.* Medically, this is considered physiological shock. Spiritually / energetically, it's the love / grace that guides and assists during seeming tragedies.

I've interviewed many people over the last 50 years who were shot, stabbed, or fell from great heights. All of them said it initially just felt like a punch to the involved area. After that, they reported feeling nothing. I hope this information lessens your torment that he suffered greatly. Even though he was physically speaking, his real self may have already disconnected. As such, he likely wasn't feeling what you might assume.

There is meaning behind the timing and way he changed worlds. For example, before receiving your note, I hadn't written an article about this topic. You motivated me to do so, and many people have been helped by it. Some of them will be *15%ers* so their actions can have big impacts. There probably are many more silver linings that arose from his time on earth and passing. I hope you can discover and focus on your own list.

**Q#4: My wife was murdered last year. How can you think this is a totally safe, loving, and fair universe when something like that happens?**

A#4: I'll grant you, that would block many people from realizing the truth of my statement. I understand how my views could sound like an ignorant and cruel joke to you. Let's break down that claim...

    1. *Life is totally safe.* Her energy, spirit, and consciousness cannot die. Yes, her earth-suit was killed, but that was a mere fraction of who and what she really is. That's why it's so important to

## When a Loved One's Physical Form is Murdered

look beyond outer physicality and realize she was **and is** much more than that.

2. *Life is totally loving.* This statement has been made by religious / spiritual teachers, near death experiencers, and those with expanded views such as clients of Life Between Lives(R) sessions. Love is one of the highest energies and ways of being. I heartily agree with the statements *G. O.D. is love, it's all love,* and *we are beings of love.*

3. *Life is totally fair.* This one may be the most difficult to accept so let's use the murder of her physical body as an example. I can think of at least four reasons why that may have happened to her body. (In each of these scenarios, you volunteered to play the role of the heart-broken husband. Why? Because you deeply understood *'The Great News'* – or wanted to even more – and knew the potentials for growth, learning, and service in this apparent tragedy.)

    a. She is an advanced person / soul who agreed to have her earthly body murdered. Why? So that a beginner soul with whom something is terribly wrong – imbalanced brain chemistry or severe abuse, for example – can learn that murder is not acceptable. That person will feel, perhaps while on earth but definitely during his life review, the pain and horror that murder causes others.

    b. Your wife was a murderer in another time / space setting. (The history of earth is full of violence, but no one likes to think they were a killer.) As such, she wanted to feel what it was like to have her earthly life ended by murder. Despite her history, her death wasn't punitive, it was instructive.

    c. A dear family member or friend of hers – maybe you – murdered someone in another time / space setting. He wanted to experience what it is like to have a loved one murdered. Why? So that he would be more certain to never do that again. Your wife freely volunteered to be 'the victim' because she knew *'The Great News'*.

    d. It was her time to move into the next phase of life. The murder of her earthly form provided a means for that to happen so she could return Home. She could also fulfill one of the other three possibilities above at the same time.

If I can think of four reasons this may have happened, there are probably many more. I hope this helps you at least open to the possibility that life is not as chaotic, hateful, and cruel as it sometimes appears. Perhaps you can at least glimpse that *life is totally safe, loving, and fair.*

# QUESTION SECTION #23: WHEN YOUR BODY IS DYING

When your earthly form is dying, you may experience physical pain and limitations. You may feel scared, angry, resentful, and a host of other strong lower-energy emotions. Family and friends might be very sad and unable to talk about their feelings. Health care staff might glibly say 'You're going to be OK' if they aren't personally comfortable with death. (You are going to be OK, just not on earth.) All this can make it difficult to process how you feel.

Amidst all this, I encourage you to remember that bodily death is a totally safe and natural part of life. Given the collective scientific, clinical, and firsthand experience evidence, you can justifiably release all fear about death. With a renewed focus on the positive, you can look forward to the fascinating adventures that lie ahead in other realms. Celebrating that you will be happy, healthy, and whole in the next phase of life is a new option. You can count on seeing loved ones again and having joyful reunions.

With this higher perspective, you can approach bodily death like you do any other big trip: take care of business beforehand, excitedly anticipate loved ones who will greet you, and prepare for a magnificent experience. Now that it is definitively known death is not a goodbye, you can plan and enjoy a 'see you later' party. Design how you spend the final days of this earthly experience in special ways.

The great religions have long taught that death is a door to a new and better life. For example, Hindu mystics have known through direct perception for several millennia that bodily death isn't a big deal. One great word from India for dying is 'dropping the body.' That conscious language term reflects their deep understanding that death is a relatively inconsequential event.

A story from that culture describes a wise teacher who was close to death. His students pleaded 'Oh master, don't leave us.' He opened one eye and said, 'Don't be silly. I wouldn't leave you. Where could I possibly go?' As they pressed him to share one last bit of wisdom, he said: 'Birth is thus, death is thus. Birth or death, what's the fuss?'

Humor is sorely needed about this subject since *the belief that anyone really dies is a joke.* French philosopher and historian Voltaire said God is like a comedian playing to an audience that's too afraid to laugh. I agree.

## Articles
*#7 When Your Physical Body Is Dying*

*#8 When a Loved One's Earthly Form Is Dying*

*#55 A Good Death*

*#79 Changing Worlds in Just 8 Days*

**Books:** *Soul Proof, Greater Reality Living, The Afterlife Evidence, The Big Picture of Life, The Eleven Questions*

# When Your Body is Dying

**Audio Programs:** *Life Review; Facilitated After Death Contact; A.R.T.; Ask Your Soul, G.O.D. and Angels*

**Q#1: At age 59, I have been given six months to live due to pancreatic cancer. How can I make the most of my time on earth? It's difficult when my loved ones have such long faces. I can see their fear about dying in general, and their sadness about me in particular.**

A#1: Kudos for sensing and describing that so clearly. Many people couldn't do that, so I expect you are more evolved. Definitive proof of life after death is a game changer for how we live and die. Before the proof, as many people have shared with me, there was an understandable concern: 'What if my religion is wrong?' Now people can handle the process of dying with more peace, hope, gratitude, faith, and even joy.

These higher-energy emotions / ways of being allow you to do what you love as long as you can. Walt Disney and Albert Einstein worked on key projects up until their time of passing. You don't have to cease enjoying dear ones, your lifework, or favorite hobbies just because your earth-suit is falling apart. If you're reading or hearing this, you may still have purposes to fulfill. Wonderful days are possible as you prepare to transition from earth.

As you approach bodily death consciously and calmly, you can share sacred gifts with your loved ones. Show them the clear evidence that life continues after bodily death and discuss it. Talk about how you feel and ask them to share as well. Encourage them to think of dying as very much like human birth since both prepare you for a new phase of life. *Death is a mere comma amidst a sentence in life's never-ending story.* An online search about 'conscious dying' will bring up more information about how you can design this.

Again, I salute your focus and taking the high road to this. Enjoy your new adventures.

**Q#2: Isn't 'not-knowing' for sure about life after death part of the plan? If it's OK for us to know for certain about an afterlife, why is there a veil? I don't believe in any one religion, but aren't we supposed to live by faith?**

A#2: Regarding 'not knowing', surely One Mind wants us to have as much peace, joy, love, and understanding as possible. Knowing for sure that life continues after bodily death would nurture those higher-energy emotions more than fear and sadness. *If there is indeed a set plan, might it be more about the outcome versus the detailed path?*

Regarding a veil, is there really one? Certain concepts have developed over time that aren't supported by contemporary findings. Beliefs in 'a veil' may have risen to understand how The Light ensures two things: (1) people awaken on earth in a balanced and timely way that doesn't cause mental imbalance, and (2) people are protected from imbalanced entities.

People may suffer if they expand their perceptions of reality too much too quickly. That's why I favor safe and time-tested paths to enlightenment versus mind-altering drugs. (article #64) Each day, pray / intend for shielding and protection from lower-energies and imbalanced entities. That can be achieved without a so-called veil that separates earth and other realms.

Having faith is important. However, it seems that a wise and loving Higher Power would also want people to benefit from knowledge and firsthand experience.

**Q#3: My mum is 90, has dementia, and is dying from heart and kidney failure. I feel that she is already walking between the worlds. How might I best help her?**

A#3: *Walking between the worlds.* What a lovely phrase! Bravo for being sufficiently enlightened to ask that question while your mother transitions to the next phase of forever.

I recommend several ways to assist her journey:

1. Stay peaceful and remember that she is preparing for the next stage of life. You may be the only person around her who isn't dealing with fear and other lower-energy emotions. Your calm presence can help her and others to optimally handle the transition.

2. When she seems 'out of it', talk directly into her ear since hearing may be the last sense to diminish before dying. Encourage her to see the Light, look for 'departed' loved ones, and trust in God. Use terms and stories that are familiar to her.

3. No matter what her mental status seems to be, let her know that you and other loved ones are ready for her to move on when she is. Since a mother's job is never done, she may be hanging on because she's worried about her 'little ones'.

4. When she is lucid, ask if she has sensed any 'departed' people or pets while awake or dreaming. Assure her that it is common to see postmaterial loved ones who arrive to assist her into the Light.

5. Read article #55 and discuss with other family members. Tell hospital staff if no lifesaving measures are used and provide a copy of her Living Will. Have a Power of Attorney document in

place in case it is needed to ensure that the family's wishes are carried out. There's a lot of money to be made during end-of-this-life care. You will want to protect her from suffering a loss of dignity and funds that she wants her family to inherit.

**Q#4: My eighty-year-old dad has been in a nursing home for ten years because of severe dementia and a long list of serious health problems. His blood pressure dropped severely so they resuscitated him and rushed him to an ICU. Now he's back in the nursing home, same as before. Why would they do that? Why wouldn't they just let him die with dignity?**

A#4: That is a great question, one that I wish more people would ask and take action on. We wouldn't let an animal suffer like that. Why are humans subjected to repeated life-sustaining interventions when the quality of life is clearly over? And why isn't euthanasia – **which means good death** – available for those who are hopelessly ill and ready to move on? Here are a few reasons:

1. A deep fear of death makes some people do just about anything to hold on. Sometimes family members won't let health care providers stop palliative care.

2. An over-emphasis among health care providers on saving lives irrespective of quality of life issues. Well-meaning doctors and nurses sometimes see death as an enemy, a failure, and something to be fought off at any cost

3. Money. Lots and lots of money is made by keeping people alive and needing expensive diagnostic tests and treatment. In the U.S., health care is a $3 trillion dollar per year industry. About 30 percent of Medicare expenditures are for medical treatment during the last year of life on earth. Might this situation improve as more people really know

the certainty of afterlife and demand appropriate *end-of-this-life* care?

4. A disconnect between bioethics and medical technology advances. **Just because we CAN save people in advanced stages of decline doesn't mean we should.** People deserve the right to say when enough is enough.

5. Religious doctrines because the time of dying is considered God's domain. However, what about the injudicious use of medical technology that prolongs the time of dying by resuscitating decrepit bodies? Is that God's will? What about using antibiotics to keep a hopelessly ill and very old person in a nursing home from dying of pneumonia? The Almighty's will again?

When and how to change worlds should be a person's choice – not a policy mandated by churches, government, or big business. Talk with your attorney and family members about this so your dad doesn't have to suffer more. Create a living will with clear instructions for him to not be resuscitated. Now that we know that *no one really dies,* we can approach this stage of life with more common sense and dignity.

**Q#5: Might uncertainty about life after death help us live life on earth to the fullest? Wouldn't life be too easy if we really knew that life is forever?**

A#5: Actually, good evidence indicates that people live and love more fully *after* a spiritually transformative experience that strengthens their knowing about life after death. (article #17) Uncertainty results in fear and anxiety that can make it more difficult to fully enjoy this earthly experience.

Those who are certain about the afterlife still suffer through the changes and challenges of life on earth. But that suffering is usually abbreviated and less intense. Even after enlightenment, there are still ample trials on earth.

# QUESTION SECTION #24: WHEN CONSIDERING SUICIDE

*Thoughts of suicide* are fairly common when a person is in physical, mental, and / or emotional pain. *Acting on those thoughts*, however, is a much bigger step. This earthly experience can be very, very difficult at times. **Suicidal thoughts and low lethality attempts are red flags** that *help is needed to address the underlying causes of suffering, loneliness, and hopelessness.*

I don't harshly judge those who choose to end their earthly experience. Likewise, good evidence shows that E.L.G.O.D. and higher-energy assistants do NOT condemn that action. Ultimately, it's a person's choice; if someone really wants to take that step, no one can stop them. However, *unless you are extremely old and / or severely ill or disabled, things can almost always get better.* That's why I encourage people to choose other options versus suicide.

Note: Excellent resources for those considering suicide are on the What About Suicide? page under Resources at EbenAlexanderMD.com. Recommended websites include: Suicide Prevention Lifeline, The National Suicide Prevention Resource Center, American Foundation for Suicide Prevention, and LGBT Resources.

### Articles
*#5 When You Are Considering Suicide*

*#12 Holistically Fine Tuning Yourself*

*#26 Holistic Solutions for 'Mental' Symptoms*

*#36 Suicide: Core Causes and Holistic Solutions*

*#64 Drugs, Alcohol, and Greater Reality Living*

*#87 Natural Health Care*

**Books:** *Radiant Wellness*, *Soul Proof, The Big Picture of Life,*

**Audio Programs:** *Holistic Breathing; Facilitated After Death Contact; Ask Your Soul, G.O.D. and Angels*

## Q#1: If afterlife realms are so great, why not choose suicide to be there sooner?

A#1: That's *usually not the highest-energy choice* to make for several reasons:

1. The quality of your afterlife experience is determined – among other factors – by your predominant thoughts, words, and actions at your time of passing. The mental state of many who choose suicide is confusion, hopelessness, guilt, anger, and shame. Does this sound like an optimal way to start a new phase of life? The act of suicide can be emotionally and physically daunting. Again, this is not a great way to launch the next part of eternity.

2. Ending your earthly experience by suicide may deeply hurt and traumatize others.

3. Terminating your time on earth may not honor important 'soul contracts'.

## When Considering Suicide

4. Those who purposely end this earthly experience may elect to repeat similar challenges in another similar incarnation. So why not work through it this time around?

5. Much forethought usually goes into designing and implementing the many facets of your earthly visit. Why not 'finish writing / reading the book' and see how your story plays out?

6. It's been said that a long waiting list exists for those who want an earthly incarnation. Why hit the reset button when you are finally here?

7. Those who pass on by suicide may require a long period of rest and recharging. As such, those who 'tough it out' on earth may actually enjoy being with beloved PMPs sooner than those who hasten their bodily death.

If I can think of 7 reasons why suicide may not be the best option, there are likely many more.

**Q#2: I lost my son recently. I'm sure we were soulmates. I am ready to be with him and have considered ending my life. What are your thoughts about that?**

A#2: You are obviously conflicted about this, or you wouldn't have contacted me. Many parents initially feel like you do so your feelings are common and natural. Thoughts about suicide almost always lessen over time, and parents are very glad they didn't act on them. This can be your experience as well. To learn more and gain a marvelous support team, join *Helping Parents Heal* and use their free *Caring Listeners* service.

Please review the list of seven reasons above why suicide likely isn't the highest path for you. Also, remember that you receive more assistance, guidance, and support from angels, guides, and The Light than you can imagine. (articles #71 and 73)

Ending your earthly experience will take you to an afterlife realm, but it may not initially be the same joyous experience as for those who completed their earthly race. As mentioned in #7 above – **but it bears repeating** – *a reunion with your son might actually be delayed* because of passing by suicide. Why? You will quite probably need a period of rest, reorientation, and healing before you can enjoy high level interactions with soulmates and others. This isn't punitive, it's just a predictable consequence of entering the next part of life from a lower-energy state.

Lower-energy emotions that often exist before suicide can carry over into the next phase of life. Evidential mediums have relayed messages from those who passed on by suicide. Those persons sometimes express remorse for not trying other options and apologize for hurting loved ones. These feelings are not the peace, joy, and love reported by most people who transition in ways other than suicide.

I understand that you want to be with your son who has transitioned from earth. However, this could be **a spiritual set-up**, a pre-designed plan to help you and others. For example, some people / souls have a tendency to leave earth when things get tough. Your son's passing could have been *a pre-planned chance* for you to persevere and create a happier ending to this story. If that is the case, choosing non-suicide options will honor the role your son played in creating this opportunity.

His *seemingly premature passing* may have created more growth, service, and learning than if he lived for 100 years on earth. And you, as a soul / being of consciousness, may have agreed to participate in this plan. You knew that your human / emotional heart would feel like it would break. However, you also knew that **your energetic / spiritual heart could expand and open more than ever**. And that, in turn, would help you and others in many lasting ways.

If you want to choose a higher road than suicide, I recommend the following:

## When Considering Suicide

1. Call the suicide prevention hotlines and visit websites listed at the top of this section.

2. Share your feelings with your holistic health care team and get the help you need.

3. If you are on any medications, especially anti-depressants, ask your health care providers about potential side-effects of increased suicidal ideation.

4. Read articles #5, 12, 26, 36, and 87.

5. Read *Radiant Wellness* to learn how to fine-tune your body, brain, and consciousness.

6. When you feel ready, use the audio programs listed above.

**Q#3: I've followed your work for years and love what you teach. However, I've struggled with extreme depression, anxiety, and financial stress for so long. I took anti-depressants, received counseling, went to church, changed jobs, reached out to family, met new friends, etc. But nothing has helped. I started having more suicidal thoughts with the anti-depressants. I just want to cease to exist. Your thoughts?**

A#3: I hope you listen to my recommendations and follow through with action steps. If you have followed my work for years, you are quite likely more evolved than most. You may be *a 15%er* who holds so much promise but is struggling to stay balanced while on earth. **Our world needs more people like you, not fewer.** And you deserve to feel happy, healthy, and energetic again. Since you reached out, let's dive into the holistic healing waters...

Solving tough cases like yours is like opening a safe: the right combination and order of correct numbers is needed to unlock it. Use the resources listed under A#1 and A#2. If you haven't already, assemble a holistic health care team as described in article #87. Some medical treatments, as you have discovered, can make symptoms worse and don't get to the root causes. Wise physicians know that *symptoms are clues to what imbalances need addressed.*

Nutritional healing approaches like Nutrition Response Testing or Applied Kinesiology can help your body heal itself. ***I've helped many more 'mental' symptoms – depression, anxiety, panic, suicidal thoughts, etc. – with these methods than I ever did with talk therapy.*** Your brain and hormonal organs are likely imbalanced and fatigued. A real food way of eating with specific whole food supplements and herbs can likely help those organs *regain normal functioning.*

As that happens, you will begin feeling happy and peaceful again. I've seen it many times and so have other great practitioners of these methods. Many suicidal people have re-entered the flow of life after using these Safe, Affordable, Natural, and Effective (SANE) methods. I'd love to hear that you are on that list.

**Q#4: *I read about your Facilitated After Death Contact technique. I really need to contact my sister to the point that I almost want to kill myself just to see her. I know that may sound insane, but I am in a lot of pain and missing her.***

A#4: It doesn't sound insane. Your 'I almost want to kill myself' statement is an expression of your pain and missing her. Please read my answers above and use the recommended resources.

Using the Facilitated ADC technique to communicate with her may not work well now. Why? Because there is such a disconnect between your current energies of sadness, loneliness, and despair compared to her likely ones of joy, peace, and love. It would be like trying to listen to music on radio station 109.4 FM when your radio is set at 94.2 AM. Your job right now is survival and getting through this crisis. Later, when you are more stable, read article #9 to learn more about enjoying visits with your beloved sister.

**Q#5: Frankly, I am considering suicide after my wife's passing. I have read all the afterlife evidence, but don't feel like I have internalized it. It feels like the only time we can have a peaceful life without unfair bad things happening is after we die.**

A#5: I understand your feelings and have received many similar notes. Please see my answers and recommendations above. Pay special attention to the part about the likelihood that *you may see your wife sooner if you don't resort to suicide.*

Bravo for recognizing *the difference between reading and internalizing the afterlife evidence.* Dr. Schwartz and I wrote *Greater Reality Living* so people could move beyond a superficial and intellectualized knowing about life after death. The power of a deep inner knowledge was captured by this statement attributed to Jesus: "And ye shall know the truth, and the truth shall make you free."

When you really know 'The Great News', this earthly experience becomes a whole new ballgame. You see life with new eyes and realize that **having inner peace and joy is an inside job**. Feeling that way isn't guaranteed after your earthly form dies. As things stand, you might haul your old beliefs and feelings with you. Those may take a while to refute and upgrade; you can do that now, so why wait? Then you can make a more informed and balanced decision about whether to end this earthly experience.

Your perception of reality is skewed right now after your wife's passing. As you said, 'It *feels* like...' Other ways of saying that would be 'It seems as though...' and 'It appears that...' These statements recognize that *you're not seeing things clearly right now.* To paraphrase Unity ministers Eric Butterworth and James D. Freeman: 'Your job is not so much to *set* things right as it is to *see* things rightly.'

With less work than you might expect, you can someday feel like this man...

> The love of my life passed away after suffering for years with extreme pain. I missed her so much that I wanted to join her but wouldn't for the sake of family and friends. My faith collapsed so much that I had serious doubts I would ever be with her again. Your positive knowledge that *no one really dies* lifted me out of my depression. Now I talk to my darling wife every day and can feel her presence. Thank you so much for helping me feel peace now and when it's my time to pass on.

Notes like this are one reason I work so hard and long to help those who can't yet see the big picture of life. I'd love to hear that you chose a similar high-energy path.

# QUESTION SECTION #25: OPTIMALLY HANDLING SUFFERING

During six years of working part-time in hospitals as a respiratory therapist, I worked with many heartbreaking cases and many people who died. Little children who were fatally hit by cars or abused. Young athletes who one moment were playing football and the next completely paralyzed. A woman who was raped and had her neck slit and left for dead. People literally suffocating to death after many years of smoking cigarettes.

We tried to help some who were shot, and others who shot themselves. I worked with people who were stabbed, molested, and had limbs amputated. Others were trapped in burning buildings or fell from great heights. Many paraplegics and quadriplegics. Brain damage so severe that the people ended up in vegetative comas with shriveled shells of bodies

Since then, I've worked as a counselor and holistic chiropractic physician for 44 years with many people who suffered with a variety of challenges. *In my personal life*, dear relatives and friends have suffered and died. Relationships have ended and my heart sometimes felt like it would burst. I endured big financial losses, broken dreams, physical injuries, severe hearing loss, and aging changes.

*Welcome to life on planet earth.* So much richness, beauty, and opportunity mixed with so many changes and challenges. However, as an old saying goes: 'You can't stop the birds of suffering from flying over your head, but you can prevent them from nesting in your hair.' (View my photo to see the humor behind that saying for me.) The point? **Even while you encounter difficulties, you don't have to suffer excessively or for a long time.** You can always choose how you respond to adversity.

## Articles

*#10 Optimally Handling Life's Biggest Changes and Challenges*

*#11 Expanding Your View of Life*

*#29 Suffering: Optimally Handling Life's Changes and Challenges*

*#40 The Love, Acceptance, and Forgiveness Technique*

*#49 When You Have Been Abused: How to Heal and Transform*

*#50 Choosing Action Over Discouragement*

*#53 When You Encounter Loss*

*#58 It's Just a Game: Optimally Handling Life's Biggest Challenges*

*#59 Follow the Silver Lining Road*

*#67 Contrast Souls*

*#70 Holistic Breathing Technique*

*#84 Heal and Transform Your Suffering Technique*

**Books:** *Soul Proof, Greater Reality Living, The Eleven Questions, The Big Picture of Life*

**Audio Programs:** *Holistic Breathing; Heal and Transform Your Suffering; Pre-Birth Planning; A.R.T. Technique; Ask Your Soul, G.O.D. and Angels*

## Optimally Handling Suffering

***Q#1: I've heard the sayings 'Suffering is bliss' and 'Suffering is grace' but they sound like nonsense to me. What am I missing?***

A#1: I felt the same way when I heard these as a young man. Now, at age 68, I understand those sayings for the following reasons:

    1. Some people tend to 'major in minors.' They get sidetracked by relatively unimportant matters such as what Hollywood star got married or a multi-billionaire's new yacht. Some live vicariously through others instead of reaching their highest potentials. *Without big challenges, they might remain stuck in spiritual amnesia.* Suffering is a blessing because it can shake us up and motivate us to search for sensible answers to life's biggest questions.

    2. Suffering can lead to more empathy and compassion for others. Looking back on my nearly seven decades in this earthly body, I see that my greatest difficulties helped me grow, serve others, and enjoy amazing adventures. To paraphrase Garth Brooks in *The Dance:* 'I could have missed the pain, but I would have missed the dance.'

I invite you to read the articles and use the audio products above. Then spend some quiet time and reconsider those sayings. In my cosmology, The Divine designed huge blessings – bliss and grace – amidst struggles and suffering. Are you ready to look for the silver linings and create a better life for you, others, and our planet?

***Q#2: I pray for many people and pets, but my prayers seem to be a waste of time. Do you really believe in prayer and, if so, why?***

A#2: If you only look at life with your physical eyes, I can understand why you question the power of prayer. You didn't say what you pray for so that could be part of the issue. If you pray for loved ones to be immune to disease and death, you set yourself up for disappointment since those conditions are part of the earthly experience. To see my prayers, read article #89.

Heartwarming stories from near death experiencers validate that the energy behind prayers can actually be seen or felt. One woman who was visiting The Light saw beautifully colored streams of light pulsating outwardly from earth. When she inquired about them, she was told 'Those are prayers being sent by people on earth for those who recently passed on.'

Another woman had an NDE after a near-fatal auto accident. As her awareness hovered above the car and watched her earthly form being resuscitated, she could *hear and feel* the thoughts of people in passing cars. Most complained because the wreck ensnarled traffic. But one man sent out prayers, love, and well wishes for people in the accident and emergency workers. Still in her out-of-body state, the woman noted the license plate of the car. After her long recovery in the hospital, the woman found the address of the man who sent out prayers. She visited his house with flowers and acknowledged the power of those high-energy thoughts he sent out.

I hope this story helps you, as it did me, realize how very real and impactful prayers are.

During religious services of my youth, I heard the following words attributed to St. Paul: "Rejoice at all times. Pray without ceasing. Give thanks in every circumstance, for this is God's will for you in Christ Jesus." At the time, I thought 'Pray without ceasing'? You've got to be kidding me. Many years later, I talk to and listen to Source every day as much as I can: before yoga and meditation, while driving, in spare moments, and before going to sleep. **Prayer – along with being joyful, peaceful, and grateful – is a powerful**

***combination***. That is a time-tested formula for enjoying a heavenly life now and after your body dies.

The *content* of your prayers is important. As a child, I was taught a horrible prayer: *'Now I lay me down to sleep. I pray the Lord my soul to keep. If I should die before I wake, I pray the Lord my soul to take.'* My primary complaints about this?

    a. The implied untrustworthy nature of the Divine. Would 'He' keep my soul if I forgot to pray? What about if 'He' was in a bad mood or just forgot?

    b. Is the 'If I should die before I wake' part supposed to comfort a child?

    c. Might 'the Lord' not take my soul if I don't pray for that each night?

No wonder so many people live with fear and reject any notion of a Higher Power!

Some reasons why your prayers may not have the desired impact:

    1. *Your energy behind the prayers* is of a lower vibration. I'm not saying yours are like that, but prayers from fearful and angry persons are lower-energy communications. You know how to upgrade those over time.

    2. *What you pray* for may not be in highest alignment for you, the people, and pets.

    3. You might benefit from listening more after prayers. It's been said that prayers are talking to Source and meditating is listening. See articles # 51, 77, and 86 to learn how to quiet your brain and improve your communication with All That Is.

## Q#3: With all the suffering in the world, how can you say that life is fair?

A#3: I make that statement based on the evidence and understandings shared throughout this book. The average material person's perception of reality is so limited that the five senses can't gauge if life is fair or not. Recall the estimates from top physicists that if all existence on earth were the size of Mt. Everest, the average person can only perceive a golf-ball sized portion. As such, we should pause before judging what is fair and what is not. Many common beliefs are based on limited understandings compiled from millennia of looking through a tiny pinhole in a wall. No wonder life doesn't make sense and seem fair at times.

When asked what the most important message he could share was, legendary architect, systems theorist, and philosopher Buckminster Fuller said: 'The universe is friendly.' Much evidence and many wise people agree. To gain a more expansive and trusting view of life, read the articles and use the audio programs listed above. To paraphrase Alan Watts, those will help you: 'G*et out of your brain and come to your senses'.*

## Q#4: As a youth, I was abused sexually, physically, and mentally. How am I supposed to lead a normal life after all that?

A#4: One day at a time with a vision of becoming stronger *not despite but because of* that abuse. A surprisingly number of people, especially women, have been similarly abused. Some identify themselves as a helpless victim for the rest of their days: PTSD diagnosis, disability, needing a comfort animal, etc. **I'm not criticizing. I am saying there is another way.**

Rev. Geraldine, a dear friend who changed worlds at age 80, was a sterling example of how early abuse doesn't have to ruin your life.

*It can, in fact, transform your life for the better.* Raped by an uncle at age fourteen, she became pregnant, and her family threw her out on the streets. A long and difficult path led to her becoming a superb minister, inspirational speaker, and healer. While speaking to a group shortly before passing on, she said she wouldn't change what happened during her teens even if she could. Why? Because that adversity helped her develop such inner strength that, in turn, helped so many people.

NOW would be a great time to search for and apply the benefits to your abuse. Read the articles and use audio sessions listed above to get a great start. When you catch yourself thinking, speaking, and acting like a helpless and pitiful victim, upgrade those to higher-energy ones. Post positive intentions where you will see and read them often. For example: *'I survived abuse and am stronger because of it. I am finding and sharing the silver linings with others.'* See article #49 to learn more about healing and transforming after being abused.

**Q#5: I have suffered a lot in my life with different diseases and now am disabled. How can I find blessings to what seems to be bad luck or a karmic curse?**

A#5: Kudos for asking this question. *The quality of your life depends, in part, upon the quality of your questions.* Some people in your situation would ask, 'Why me?' 'Is there really a God?' or other disempowering questions. To find the blessings...

    1. Follow recommendations in answers above.

    2. Use the *Ask Your Soul, G.O.D. and Angels* technique to access your inner knowing and guidance from Source and your higher-energy assistants. (article #71)

3. After saying your prayers, *ask Universe: 'How can I serve?'* Then keep your eyes and heart open. That may be praying for others and sending them healing energy. Despite being very infirm, my aunt Dottie did this until she was 94 years old. Consider other times of adversity that you have successfully navigated and realize how resilient and resourceful you are. You might write articles or blogs about your journey through the dark night of the soul and what you've learned. Or you could assist others with multiple physical problems about staying focused on the blessings.

4. *Develop a greater reality perspective.* This earthly experience, even if you live to 100, is a blink of an eye in the span of forever. Remember the distinct possibility that **only part of you – your energy / lifeforce / awareness is physically disabled**. Thus, much of who you really are may be simultaneously enjoying robust wellness now. This part of you and your soulmates are cheering you on to remember the big picture of life and handle your challenges with style.

5. *Don't judge too soon.* Your diseases and disabilities might prepare you for very important roles in the next life. Without your struggling and searching, you wouldn't be able to serve others as well.

# Part 3: Holistic Solutions

# Question Section #26: Fine-Tuning Your Body and Brain

You are a wise, infinite, special, and powerful part of Life Itself. But it's difficult to *know and show* that if – like many people – you are depressed, fatigued, anxious, overweight, or suffering from imbalances. That's why wise persons treat their body like a temple of the soul. Optimally caring for your body allows your mind and inner light to shine through in incredible ways no matter what is happening to or around you. And that, in turn, improves your life and shows others that it is possible.

The quality of your earthly experience is greatly determined by your vitality and wellness, or lack thereof. Your time on earth is like a marathon race, not a sprint. And, as you well know, sometimes the earthly course seems all uphill. Being vibrantly healthy gives you the energy, strength, and clarity to run a good race and create the greatest life of your dreams.

## Articles
*#12 Holistically Fine Tuning Yourself*

*#32 Nutritional Based Healing*

*#33 Six Stressors*

*#37 Detoxing Chemicals and Heavy Metals*

*#43 Dirty Electricity and What You Can Do About It*

*#54 The 90 Day Program to More Energy, Clarity, and Fitness*

*#57 Immunity Enhancement Program*

*#77 Centering Practices*

*#87 Natural Health Care*

*#88 Whole Food Way of Eating and Supplements*

*#90 What Do I Eat?*

**Books:** *Radiant Wellness*

**Audio Programs:** *Your Life Review; Ask Your Soul, G. O.D. and Angels*

**Q#1: How do I remain present in the current moment with joy and gratitude when my physical body feels fatigued and overwhelmed?**

A#1: Kudos for asking that excellent question. Suboptimal beliefs, thoughts, lifestyle habits, self-care, and / or health care are usually behind fatigue and other common symptoms. Those can often be addressed with natural treatment methods and optimal self-care habits. I know this very well after helping many people over the last fifty years in various health care settings.

Recommendations for feeling more energetic and less overwhelmed...

   1. Read the articles listed above and make regular improvements. Don't try to change too much at once or it will feel like too much work and stress. Just make a few changes for a while, then use the uptick in energy and clarity to make others.

2. Nutrition-base healing approaches are so powerful in addressing fatigue, overwhelm, depression, and other common symptoms. For example, many women suffer from childbirth-related nutritional deficiencies that, over time, impair optimal functioning of the brain and hormonal organs. That's one reason why some middle-aged women suffer with so many symptoms that they are sometimes inaccurately considered hysterical by their doctor. The cause isn't in their heads. To learn more, see articles #12 and 87.

3. Read my book *Radiant Wellness* to learn seven keys to getting and staying well.

4. Regularly use *centering practices* as described in article #77. Meditate, pray, spend time in nature, and enjoy 'earthing' by prudently walking barefoot on grass, sand, or shallow water.

5. Use *Holistic Breathing* as directed to release old wounds, erroneous teachings, and needless fears. This frees up stuck energy so you feel more energized and capable to handle all of life's challenges.

6. Use the *Ask Your Soul, G.O.D. and Angels* session to access guidance about how to fine-tune yourself holistically.

Your inner self knows how to be joyful, peaceful, and clear. The steps listed above will rehab your body so your brain-based consciousness is more congruent with your transcendental source of consciousness. I hope you love yourself enough to spend the time, energy, and money to make this transformation.

### Q#2: Do you have any opinions on chakras and feng shui?

A#2: Chakras or *energy centers* have been described for millennia in Hindu, Taoist, Buddhist, Sikh, and other Eastern wisdom sources. We are beings of energy so it makes sense that there would be specific centers associated with different life emphases. The system I am most familiar with is the seven-chakra system:

#1 perineum: *survival*

#2 umbilicus: *pleasure and sensation*

#3 solar plexus: *power and mastery*

#4 middle of chest: *love*

#5 throat: *expressing your highest truths*

#6 above bridge of nose: *higher perceptions and abilities*

#7 crown of head: *cosmic consciousness,* that is, deeply knowing 'The Great News' and demonstrating it in every part of your life.

Many people on earth focus primarily on chakras #1 – 3. Chakra #4, the energetic heart / love center, is **the bridge** to *a balanced focus* on #1 – 3 AND #5 – 7.

Feng shui is another well-established practice from Eastern traditions that recognizes energy can flow smoothly and optimally, or not. The field of feng shui addresses mental and physical clutter / imbalances that can cause slower, stagnated, or blocked energy flows.

After addressing those factors, feng shui recommends favorable placement of furniture, art, plants, etc. to assist optimal energy at home and work environments. I feel and function better when living In a more simple, clean, quiet, peaceful, and organized environment.

Learning more about both subjects is wise for those seeking to fine-tune their personal energy and upgrade every aspect of their earthly experience.

**Q#3: My church teaches that the body is weak and an enemy of the soul. But, lately, this doesn't make much sense to me. Any words of wisdom about this?**

A#3: Congratulations for listening to your heart and mind instead of schizoid babble from the Dark Ages and pre-B.C. eras. What loving and wise Creator would set things up that way? Those fear-based teachings paint such a bleak picture for the prospects of people being happy and achieving success.

Why would so-called religious teachers share such ignorant and sacrilegious messages? Often because of powerful men – *women usually wouldn't teach such garbage* – who control that denomination. They establish doctrines, hold the power and wealth, and set up what ministers are taught. This system tries to control people into believing they must seek 'the one true way' which, coincidentally, that church just happens to offer. It's one of the oldest con games on earth and some people fall for it.

Actually, your body is a magnificent, powerful, and resilient miracle. It is literally made of stardust and is energized by the same power / intelligence that creates and sustains all life. My studies of human anatomy and physiology were as much a testimonial to a wondrous Creator as my theological studies.

In the late 18th century, chiropractic philosophers said that another name for 'God' was *Universal Intelligence*. Further, they posited that *all people have a spark of that* – which they termed Innate Intelligence – within. Our earthly experiences flow best when we listen to that inner wisdom. Whenever possible, addressing physical and mental symptoms should be done in conjunction with Mother Nature.

Bravo for recognizing that those teachings don't make sense. I hope you will continue to listen to your inner knowing – *that calm small voice within* – and demonstrate what your body and soul working together are capable of.

**Q#4: Some medical doctors say that natural health care is a bunch of baloney. Is that why they focus on drugs and surgery?**

A#4: I worked in hospitals, mainly ER and ICU units, for six years. Numerous family members and friends are nurses and medical doctors. I know firsthand that medical treatment is miraculous for emergencies and crises. I recommend drug, surgical, and other invasive treatment methods for broken bones, ruptured organs, injuries from accidents, stroke, and other severe conditions.

However, those **disease-care approaches have little to offer for many common symptoms, syndromes, and even named diseases**. Invasive and expensive treatments may relieve symptoms, but they don't address the underlying causes. For example, cutting out the gall bladder might alleviate GI discomfort and other symptoms. But that didn't address the sludge and small soft stones in it and associated ducts that caused the symptoms. Further, *negative potential side-effects* can occur after having body parts cut out.

In the past, many medical doctors received little or no training about natural healing methods such as chiropractic, nutrition, acupuncture, cranial adjusting, and deep tissue massage. Nearly 85% of teachers at medical schools had direct or indirect ties with the pharmaceutical industry and / or medical device makers. So guess what medical students were taught?

*Follow the money.* **The disease care industry** – hospital complexes, pharmaceutical companies, insurance companies, and medical device manufacturers – is a $3 trillion per year business in the U.S. alone. That amount of money powerfully shapes policy influencers and lawmakers. It also pays for ubiquitous advertisements that convince people to just 'ask your doctor' despite the serious side-effects quickly mentioned at the end of the ads.

Medical (allopathic and osteopathic) students now receive at least some information about natural healing approaches. I recommend that you find an *integrative medical doctor* who understands the value of holistic health care and recommends that whenever possible. First do no harm and all that.

# Question Section #27:
# Communicating with 'Departed' Loved Ones Now

Maintaining meaningful relationships with postmaterial loved ones may be less difficult than you might think. They usually are *motivated and able* to establish contact. Communicating with PMPs is much like talking by phone with those living across the world. You can't see them, but you know they are still alive.

The main difference is that you can hear the voices of material persons with your ears. While communicating with 'deceased' dear ones, you may hear them *objectively / outwardly* with your usual sense of hearing. However, hearing them *subjectively / inwardly or telepathically* is much more common.

SoulPhone communication technology is being researched and developed at the *Laboratory for Advances in Consciousness and Health* at the University of Arizona. Services and devices may one day allow texting with, talking to, and seeing those living in other realms. (articles #35,44, 85; SoulPhone.com)

Until then, you can use the resources below to enjoy continued, although different, visits with your loved ones who have graduated from earth-school.

## Articles
*#6 Evidential Mediums*

*#9 Visiting 'Departed' Loved Ones Now*

*#28 After Death Communications*

*#51: Meditation and Relaxation Techniques*

**Books:** *Greater Reality Living, Soul Proof*

**Audio Programs:** *Holistic Breathing, Facilitated ADC*

## Q#1: Can my dear ones who passed on know when I talk to or think intensely about them?

A#1: Postmaterial communication does not appear to be limited by time or space. So, yes, your 'departed' loved ones may hear you when you talk to or think about them. I say 'may' because there is much we don't yet know about afterlife realms. For example:

    1. Are they fully rested and recharged so they can receive and transmit messages?

    2. Is their energy / awareness needed in another time-place right now? If so, that might preclude being aware of you and sending signs. (That may not be a factor if they are already adept at multilocation.)

    3. Did your 'soul contract' design opportunities for postmaterial communication? Or might your and / or their evolution proceed better without that?

To date, several well-run scientific experiments with postmaterial collaborators indicate that their consciousness can 'travel' across the country nearly instantaneously. In my opinion, there is no significant veil or barrier between earth and other realms. If you go far enough into outer space, you won't eventually see a sign that says, 'Warning, don't crash into the veil!' or 'You are now approaching *The Other Side*.' My point? You and your loved ones may be much closer than you might imagine. Continuing a relationship with dear ones is possible no matter where they live.

**Q#2: My daughter changed worlds recently. How soon might she be able to communicate with me via an ADC or through a medium?**

A#2: I am sorry for your pain and suffering but glad you are already exploring how to stay in touch with her. There are a few factors that determine when she might be ready to do that:

**Regarding her...**

1. Is she a beginner, intermediate, or advanced soul / energy / person?

2. What was her physical and mental state just before crossing over? Healthy, joyful, and peaceful? Or very ill, depressed, and fatigued?

3. How did she pass on? For example: (a) peacefully while surrounded by loved ones so she was prepared for transitioning, or (b) violently and suddenly after an impulsive suicide.

4. Is she rested, recharged, reoriented, and focused on higher energies now?

5. Is she able to attempt interdimensional communication and is that her intention?

6. Is she involved with high priority activities in the next realm that require her focus?

**Regarding you...**

1. Similar questions about #1 and 4 apply to you.

2. Are you seeking contact from a balanced, peaceful, and curious state of mind? Or are you more anxious, fearful, and demanding?

**Regarding the medium(s),** are they...

1. highly skilled and experienced?

2. rested, healthy, and balanced?

3. having 'a good day'?

Another factor about mediums is their belief system about the optimal time for attempting contact. Top mediums who have been evaluated under double blind conditions differ in their answers about this. Some say it's better to wait at least six months before seeking a reading. Others say it might work right after passing.

My guestimate is that it takes a month or two for a 'departed' loved one to make contact. Why? After embracing The Light and enjoying a reunion with postmaterial loved ones, there's usually a healing and recharging period. Then newly arrived people rejoin their groups and get reoriented. Time on earth and the next realm might seem quite different so 4 – 8 weeks in earth-time might seem very brief to postmaterial persons.

**Q#3: My mom died five years ago. There was so much I wanted to say to her and now it's too late. Can she still hear me?**

A#3: With much love and respect, *your mom didn't really die*. Only her earthly body did. As such, it's never too late to convey your deepest feelings and thoughts to her.

Many people have enjoyed meaningful communications with postmaterial loved ones using methods described in articles #6 and 9. Conversations proceed best when both parties are 'on the line'. She most likely is willing and able to talk and listen. As such, it may be more a matter of you *believing it's possible, being receptive, and practicing*.

**Ten keys to visiting with postmaterial loved ones...**

1. Deeply internalize the evidence that death is not a goodbye, just a 'see you later'.

2. Pray / intend that you will have contact with her if, all things considered, that is best.

3. Get on a higher-energy wavelength via meditation, time in nature, prayer, service to others, healthy diet, exercise, expressing gratitude, etc.

4. Be aware of subtle communications, electronic aberrations, animal signs, and mysterious events. Realize that her contact may not necessarily arrive how and when you expect.

5. Talk to her as if she is present since she probably is.

6. Ask her questions aloud or silently, and then listen with your head and heart.

7. Realize it may not be easy at first for you two to communicate. Relax and don't put any pressure on either of you.

8. Hold an object of hers since residual energy might enhance a connection.

9. Give thanks when any communication happens so it's more likely to happen again.

10. Leave room for the "X" factor since there's much we don't know about life.

### Q#4: Why don't I feel the calming presence of my loved ones who have passed on?

A#4: They may be trying to make their presence known, but you aren't detecting it. Some people have a preconceived notion of what an otherworldly visit looks or feels like. Centering practices help quiet your brain so you can sense when postmaterial loved ones are nearby. (#77)

I recommend reading the articles listed above and using the ten keys in A#3. Then use the two audio programs listed in that order. *Holistic Breathing* sessions can help you release lower-energy emotions and wounds that may block your perception of postmaterial loved ones. After a month of that, the *Facilitated ADC* technique will likely be more productive.

Now that it's definitively demonstrated scientifically that no one really dies, you can relax and release needless fears. That simple act may increase your awareness of 'departed' loved ones who are very near.

### Q#5: Recently, our son's car hit a tree and he died on the spot. Our thirteen-year-old daughter communicated with him telepathically soon after. Through her, he described

***a squabble with a friend in the car that caused the accident. That friend refused to talk to us and left the country. Should we believe this based on our daughter's conversations with him?***

A#5: Only you can decide what to believe. Some siblings, especially those who were very close on earth, receive clear communications from a 'departed' brother or sister fairly soon. Perhaps your son did explain what happened through her. An evidential medium session might confirm what she reported. (article #6)

It's common for parents to search for clues about how and why their child passed on. Early in the grief process, this form of denial or bargaining may be adaptive. However, a 'psychological autopsy' can become unhealthy if you spend too much time and energy on it.

Whether that is what really happened or not, your son has passed on. Please focus on grieving fully and getting recharged and re-balanced. Read article #2 and take action steps. When you feel ready, read the articles and use the audio programs listed above to develop different but meaningful communication with him. That will flow best if you're focused on higher-energy emotions versus investigating whether his friend was involved in the accident.

**Q#6: I know my loved ones who have died are really alive and well. I get that. They're just in another world or dimension. Can they visit more often during the holidays? I've had several loved ones cross over this year and it's going to be tough.**

A#6: Kudos for knowing that bodily death is a natural passage to another dimension of life. Much firsthand experience indicates that postmaterial loved ones DO visit more during anniversaries and holidays. (To learn about this, see lesson #15 in article #93.) They are still part of the family and want to continue being close. They also know it can be more difficult for those on earth, so they try to share signs that they are near.

Have you invited them to visit more during special times? Just send that invitation out however you like. Have you taken steps to better **perceive their visits and feel their comfort?** To start, read the articles above and use the audio techniques. Focus on the ten keys listed under A#3 to detect their visits. Over time and with practice, those resources will likely amplify your ability to sense them. With more certainty that life and love continue, you can relax into the flow of life and do what you came here to do: love, serve, grow, learn, enjoy, and have adventures.

**Q#7: Three months ago, I lost my very dear older sister. I just can't get over my grief and sadness. How can I communicate with her now or get a message from her?**

A#7: Same answer as A#6. However, you will also need to expand your knowing that, as the last person stated: "*I know my loved ones who have died are really alive and well. I get that. They're just in another world or dimension.*"

A deeper knowing about that and *Holistic Breathing* sessions can help release your deep grief and sadness. And that, in turn, will allow you to extend your senses and perceive your dear one who is quite likely trying to reach her kid sister.

**Q#8: My mom was a very wise soul and we were very close. Recently, she passed on at an advanced age after suffering with Alzheimer's. I looked forward to feeling her presence more, but the opposite is true. I don't feel her at all except just during some dreams. I understand**

now when people say death seems so final. What are your suggestions about this?*

A#8: Here are a few reasons why this may be happening:

   1. Since her passing was fairly recent, she may still be in the rest, recharge, and reorientation phase. This might be especially likely given her age and Alzheimer's.

   2. Because you two were / are very close, she knows that you may prefer but don't *need* immediate visits. Perhaps others family and friends who have more fear and anxiety about death need her comfort and contact more.

   3. Given that she was a very wise soul, she may be needed in the next realm.

   4. She may visit while you sleep and your brain is quieter. Dream ADCs with validation and evidential aspects show that those can be *actual visits*. They may be more than 'just dreams'. Set an intention to detect and remember her dream time visits. That may 'prime the pump' and enable more waking contact, especially when using tips in A#3.

Knowing these possible reasons can help you relax and trust that – all things considered – contact will occur if, when, and how it is meant to be. Read the articles and use the sessions to gain even more peace about this new stage of your relationship with your dear mom.

*Q#9: My husband changed worlds two years ago and I have had many signs from him. I talk to him every day and feel I can hear him. However, a very religious person told me it is not my husband sending me signs or talking to me. She referred to a scriptural passage saying 'The dead know nothing.' I am utterly distraught because knowing he is around me has helped me get through all this. I need some reassurance it is not just my imagination.*

A#9: There is a vast amount of scientific, clinical, and experiential evidence that clearly shows those who pass on can contact us.

It is a historical fact that 'holy books' have been changed over millennia via purposeful deletions, additions, translations, and interpretations. In addition, these books have been altered by intentional and unintentional transcriptions by scribes before printing presses existed. Some of those changes were designed by religious and political authorities to scare, control, and get money from fearful congregants.

The phrase 'the dead know nothing' is found in Ecclesiastes 9:5 and is usually quoted out of context. That statement also contradicts other passages in the Old and New Testaments that indicate consciousness continues after bodily death. Examples of those include Matthew 25:46, Luke 16: 19 – 31, and Ecclesiastes 4:2

Solomon, the supposed author of this *Old Testament* book, was referring to the perspective of people on earth who have no knowledge of Creator. Solomon's use of the phrase 'under the sun' about 30 times makes it clear that he was commenting on *how things appear from a limited earthly perspective*. Those who don't have a relationship with The Divine believe that 'the dead know nothing', that is, that nothing exists after bodily death.

That phrase has been used to support, without corroborating evidence, the following opinions:

1. Nothing exists after death.

2. Consciousness ceases after death until a resurrection and judgment day.

3. Only those who believe in and follow 'the one true way' experience an afterlife.

Based on the collective evidence and many religious teachings, I hope you continue to enjoy a continuing relationship with your dear husband.

**Q#10: My father passed away recently. Immediate family members have sensed him at the same time even when we are at different locations. What could it mean?**

A#10: It can be a demonstration that *consciousness is nonlocal, that is, not restricted by time and space.* Review Question Section #12 about multilocation to recall the potential for **simultaneous time-space activities**. I've heard similar reports but not that often. My sense is that only evolved and / or very dynamic PMPs can achieve that so soon after passing.

**Q#11: You say we will see loved ones again when we transition. But what if we don't want to see them again? What if they were abusive or just not the kind of person we want to be with? Even if we do love them, we may not want to be with them in our new abode.**

A#11: Great distinction. I should say 'you **can** see loved ones' instead of 'you **will**.' No one is forced to continue relationships if that isn't mutually desired. Relationships in the hereafter may be similar to those on earth. You may want to live with special loved ones all the time. With other friends and family, an occasional visit might be sufficient. And for some, it would be too soon if you never saw them again.

Regarding abusive persons, you don't have to be around them in the hereafter. But there's an important distinction. While on earth, you can only sense a fraction of who and what a person really is. Your decision about continuing an afterlife relationship, or not, may change when you experience and remember their true nature. The abusive person may actually be a soulmate who, upon your request, played that role to motivate and awaken you. To learn more about the possible blessings of *contrast souls*, see article #67.

**Q#12: What should I do if I encounter a sign from a passed loved one? Just acknowledge it or something else?**

A#12: A sign from a postmaterial loved one can launch the beginning of *a new and different type of relationship.* It can spark a spiritually transformative experience that radically alters your life for the better. Depending on what feels right, you could:

1. acknowledge the sign.

2. express gratitude for the contact.

3. inquire if there is a message and then listen / feel for a response.

4. clarify if you would like more contacts.

5. use the Facilitated ADC technique to visit regularly.

6. use the heightened energy from that exchange to improve all aspects of your life.

# QUESTION SECTION #28: GREATER REALITY LIVING

The term *greater reality living* invites you to consider: how might you live and treat others as you become more aware of **the totality of life**? Now that you know *'The Great News'*, will you think, speak, and act differently? How can you enjoy the greatest life of your dreams while on earth? (That isn't being selfish because others will benefit when you are happy and shining as brightly as possible.)

I pose these questions because **what greater reality living looks like will vary greatly**. Everyone is unique and has special reasons for being on earth at this time. A bottom line? You can enjoy the most wonderful life that you – as a timeless being of energy / consciousness – have envisioned. The information and resources I share can help you do that.

I can't overemphasize how important it is to learn and internalize *'The Great News'*. You'll recall that that these statements are most probably true and accurate based on collective afterlife evidence and contemporary understandings about the greater reality. They are fundamental to seeing the big picture of life and living accordingly.

**Articles**
*#12 Holistically Fine Tuning Yourself*

*#17 Internalizing Your Spiritually Transformative Experiences*

*#18 LGBTQI and Spirituality*

*#50 Choosing Action Over Discouragement*

*#51 Meditation and Relaxation Techniques*

*#63 All Lives Matter*

*#69 Great News Despite the Pandemic and Other Challenges*

*#72 Greater Reality Living*

*#74 Is Your Life Unfolding Perfectly?*

*#76 Twelve Experiences, Many Lessons*

*#77 Centering Practices*

*#82 Journey from 'Bereaved' to 'Shining Light'*

*#100 Enlightenment*

*#101 When Reaching a Fork in Your Life's Road*

**Books:** *Greater Reality Living, The Big Picture of Life, The Eleven Questions, Radiant Wellness*

**Audio Programs:** *Holistic Breathing; Life Review; A.R.T. Technique; Ask Your Soul, G.O.D. and Angels*

**Q#1: Your article about gay people and spirituality truly spoke to me since I am a gay man. I was raised in a very strict and closed-minded religious upbringing. God was**

*to be feared and I did not question anything. Thanks to your writings, I realize my Higher Power is loving and accepting. I forgave myself and released shame for things I have done. What are some practical steps I can take to keep progressing?*

A#1: I am honored to be part of your awakening. Some religious denominations have done such a poor job of teaching about The Source. They spew fear and have a long list of supposed sins including being gay. What a horrible disservice such 'churches' do to these special and beloved children of The Divine. Congratulations for realizing that She is loving, accepting, and couldn't consider sending any of Her children to fiery punishment forever.

I agree with the long title of an old Curtis Mayfield song: *If there's a hell below, we're all going to go.* Which among us is without sin? Who hasn't fallen down and made mistakes while learning how to do and be better?

An original Aramaic meaning for the word 'sin' was *to miss the mark*. We miss the mark when we don't love, respect, and appreciate ourselves and others. The word 'repent' meant: *Say you are sorry, make amends, and do better the next time.*

Practical steps to enjoy higher-energy feelings and ways of being are discussed throughout this book. I recommend using the four audio products listed above in that order. That should significantly increase the quality of your life and outreaches. Then you can look around and see how to evolve even more. That, to me, is a big part of heavenly living: keep learning, growing, enjoying, and serving. There is no ceiling to that process until, if desired, to merge with The One. A gender-adjusted line from Robert Browning comes to mind: 'Your reach should exceed your grasp, or what's a heaven for?

## Q#2: How can those who are awakening protect animals from mistreatment?

A#2: It can feel heartbreaking to see animals suffer. Kudos for recognizing that *15%ers* can make huge improvements in every area of life on earth including this one. Animals that provide meat are often treated inhumanely by Big Agra industries. One solution is to only buy pasture-raised meat from places where animals are slaughtered as humanely as possible. Another is to become an ovo-lacto vegetarian or vegan so no animals are killed. I quit eating meat many years ago. My occasional intake of eggs and dairy are only from *pasture-raised* animals with organic feed. (article #90)

On this planet, so much money is wasted on extravagances, needless wars, excess profits, corruption, waste, etc. A fraction of that would pay for birth control to decrease the number of strays. Pets without a home could receive great care from shelters until homes are found.

Depending on their levels of consciousness, animals may know 'The Great News' to varying degrees. With a deeply internalized knowledge of those insights, the decision to possibly suffer to experience a different facet of life AND serve others is an easy one. For example, my neighbor who is a veterinarian said pet sales and adoptions skyrocketed during Covid. (articles #22 and 39)

A dear Native American friend of mine studied with elders of different tribes around the U.S. Independently, a number of them told him that animals have *give-aways* and special gifts to share. Animals are willing to help people live on earth so both animals and people can deepen their relationship with Great Spirit. Centuries ago, this willingness to help was especially apparent during times of severe weather and unsuccessful hunting. Some animals, it was reported, would walk up to hunters, raise their head, and allow their throats to be cut so people could live.

I don't know if these stories are true or not. But they suggest that at least some animals can express a higher degree of love, awareness, and service than many humans. Animals deserve to be treated with compassion, respect, and love as do all people, plants, and nature.

**Q#3: I lost my mother to cancer. I feel like I let her down even though she didn't expect me to do all that I did and worried about me. This guilt is really making it difficult to enjoy life. How can I deal with this? Will I be able to meet her someday and say, "Sorry, Mom"?**

A#3: Oh my, some people create so much needless distress for themselves. Guilt is a lower-energy emotion that – according to David Hawkins MD, PhD, author of *Power vs. Force* – can create *a life view* that you and others are evil. Guilt can stem from *a Godview* that Creator is vindictive. This can create an 'I'll punish myself before He does' mentality. Over time, guilt and self-blame can be destructive to your physical and mental health.

Ignorant cultural and religious teachings reinforce feelings of guilt when none should exist. You felt guilty about not doing more and your mom worried about being an imposition. Your opening sentence 'I lost my mother to cancer' could be interpreted that you feel responsible for the timing of her passing. That view ignores the evidence that **meaningful timing exists for when people transition from earth**. Who is served by these lower-energy emotions and ways of living?

Your mom is – or, depending on how much rest and rehab she needed – soon will be whole, vital, and free from pain. She likely can see more of the big picture of life and has released at least some lower-energy emotions. *You now have an opportunity to do the same and enjoy greater reality living.* This book is full of information and strategies for doing that. I recommend starting with *Holistic Breathing* for a month; then add *Ask Your Soul, G.O.D. and Angels* sessions. This combination will help you get clearer and reenter the flow of life / love that surrounds you and is your truest nature. After that, you can say 'Sorry, Mom' if you want, but it won't be needed.

**Q#4: My daughter, who is gay, and I have always had a special connection. Her sexual orientation makes no difference to me: we are all souls, period. She was rejected by her father (my ex-husband) and her brother. Do souls choose to be gay to learn and experience more? Or are they influenced by other lives as the opposite sex?**

A#4: Sometimes pre-birth choices are made to be gay, or another oppressed minority, for the greater growth and service opportunities therein. LBGTQI people encounter an unbelievable amount of judgment, criticism, prejudice, hate crimes, and even murder. They knew of the potential for this, but also knew about the potential blessings from adversity. I have known many co-workers, friends, and family members who were not heterosexual. Without exception, they are among the most loving, creative, intelligent, caring, and humorous people I have known.

Religious objections to LGBTQI people are often based on the *Old Testament* story recounted in Genesis 19. You can read this curious tale and *make your own conclusions about whether it is a good source of guidance.* Different cultures have recognized LGBTQI people as unique and possibly embodying two different souls simultaneously. The term 'two spirits' was used for individuals who exhibited androgynous characteristics. Indigenous tribes, including American and Canadian Indians, recognized the special nature of these souls. (article #18)

Data from past life regressions suggests that a person who was a woman during numerous time-space experiences may carry over more feminine energies despite having a male body in this one. And vice-versa that those who were men in 'past lives' may feel more masculine energy during an incarnation in a woman's body.

This carryover may express itself in anatomy, personality, and / or preferences. Anyone who has worked in pediatric hospitals knows that a wide spectrum of male / female bodily development, organs, genetics, and feelings exist.

Souls / expressions of consciousness like to explore Life Unfolding from different observation points. Being gay provides different perspectives than being heterosexual. Likewise with having different skin color, age, religious beliefs, ethnicity, cultural upbringing, socio-economic status, etc. You know the old saying about never judging a person until you have walked a mile in their shoes? Embodying different roles allow us to do just that.

Thankfully, more people now realize and accept, as you so wisely stated: "We are all souls. Period." Any other differences are relatively trivial compared to our essential oneness and sacred interconnection with all life. This viewpoint paves the way for enhancing peace, love, appreciation, and respect for diversity and all people.

**Q#5: There are so many problems in our world that I see every day in the news. Are we nearing the end of the world?**

A#5: By 'the end of the world', I assume you mean extinction of the human race. The planet itself will survive despite all the ignorant and destructive behaviors of people. Hardy and adaptive plant and animal species may survive, and the process of evolution will continue. Thoughts to consider about the many problems in our world...

1. What *seem* like tragedies – mass murders and the pandemic, for example – may provide tickets back Home for those who don't need a long earthly experience. This viewpoint doesn't condone inappropriate behaviors, nor does it minimize the awful suffering that occurs on our planet. It does, however, remind you to consider the big picture of life.

2. Those who hurt others may be 'beginner souls' who need to learn how to not treat others. More advanced ones may actually volunteer to be hurt or killed. Why? So less evolved persons can *see, feel, and know* – while on earth and / or during their life review after crossing over – why the Golden Rule makes such good sense.

3. Difficult times can cause people to ask important questions that they wouldn't during easier ones. That provides opportunities for finding sensible answers and taking more enlightened action steps. (article #29)

4. Remember that everyone is a timeless and deathless being of energy / consciousness.

5. The list of potential benefits from challenges is beyond our comprehension.

6. If and when humanity renders itself extinct is within our control.

An old fable illustrates the last point. A foolish youth, wishing to trick a wise old man, held a little bird in his hands. 'Tell me, old man, is this bird alive or dead?' The wise one knew that if he said 'alive', the boy would crush it to death. But if he said 'dead', the youth would let it fly away. The old man said: 'Whether the bird is alive or dead is up to you.'

The same is true about the end of humanity. Will we make the planet uninhabitable by irreparably harming the air, water, and soil? Will we destroy our earthly bodies with viral, chemical, and / or nuclear weapons? It is up to us.

Many years ago, I shared your fear. I attended a talk by Swami Rama, founder of the Himalayan Institute and asked: "Are we nearing the end of the world?" He smiled slightly and said, *"Your world might end, but mine cannot."* I am concerned, but not fearful about this outcome. I do everything I can do to create peace and harmony on earth. At the same time, I remember that our essence cannot be destroyed. Hopefully, enough people are awakening to the greater reality that we will create a story with a happy ending for humanity.

Regarding the news, I don't spend too much time following that. I stay balanced and healthy, pray for peace, help as many people as possible, enjoy my beloved family and friends, and share my greatest gifts. That's enough, especially as more of us do the same.

**Q#6: My father passed on last year. The last time I saw him didn't go well. We both said things we didn't mean and it's been eating me up inside for almost a year. Any suggestions?**

A#6: I'm glad you are addressing this before your regret and guilt affect your physical and / or mental health. Your comment about *eating you up inside* suggests that could eventually manifest as an ulcer or cancer. (Remember: as you think, so shall you be.)

I know several people this has happened to, so you aren't the only one. Old men who are ill can get grumpy and start the negative comments. Use my recommendations for healing and transforming discussed in this book. Transmute the 'bad' parts of that experience to realize how precious relationships are and resolve to never let that kind of interaction happen again.

**Q#7: For a long time, I haven't been able to feel love or connection with myself and others. Since age 12, there is nothing I have been passionate about except smoking cigarettes. At age 52, I prefer to sleep than be awake. I am scared because I have not learned anything at all**

*during my time on earth. I really appreciate any guidance if you can offer any.*

A#7: Thank you for a good belly laugh. Not laughing *at you but with* the part of you that knows how ridiculous your 'I have not learned anything at all' statement is. You certainly have learned a lot, but apparently not what you want to. It's impossible to live on earth for 52 years and not be exposed to new information and experiences.

In addition, you have underestimated the power of *contrast experiences and interactions.* (article #67) You have learned very well how you **don't** want to be and feel. Your shift toward how you **do** want to be can occur more quickly, easily, and inexpensively than you might imagine.

Thanks also for your great description of how many people feel when their body / brain is out of balance. You didn't provide a history, but my sense is that you are a very loving and sensitive person who shut down because of the pain and challenges in our world. You may have experienced significant abuse, pain, and / or loss early in life and never recovered. The oral fixation aspect of smoking suggests that these wounds occurred as a child. Cigarettes also provided temporary stimulation and an energy boost so you felt a little better for a while.

*Kudos for not giving up despite 40 years of feeling disconnected and unloved!*

I hope the sadness and regret in your words motivates others who also want to turn things around. The good news? Your and their imbalances can probably be addressed with Safe, Affordable, Natural, and Effective (SANE) methods. Read articles #12, 23, 26, 32, 51, 86, 87, 88, and 90 and take incremental action steps over time. Work with a practitioner who uses nutrition-based healing via Nutrition Response Testing, Applied Kinesiology, or a similar approach.

Later, read articles #56 and 66 to develop better relationships with yourself and others. You deserve to feel healthy and happy, and the world needs your greatest gifts.

# Question Section #29: Identify and Fulfill Your Purpose

You have special gifts and talents to share. When you fulfill your purposes for being here – even just part time – this earthly experience will make more sense and feel more peaceful, joyful, and meaningful.

Realizing your true nature as a deathless being of awareness / energy bestows many gifts. One is trusting yourself enough to follow your highest callings. Knowing who you really are sets the stage for following your heart and doing what you feel called to do. Then you can increasingly trust *your intuition, that wise inner voice* that guides you about every part of your life.

My daily prayers to Source and my higher-energy assistants include, in part: *Thank you for all your love, support, guidance, and assistance as I share my greatest gifts, sing all my heart-songs, do all that I came here to do, and shine as brightly as possible.* I recommend adding your version of this intention to your daily prayers and affirmations.

**Articles**
*#21 Identify and Fulfill Your Highest Purposes*

*#65 Karma*

## Identify and Fulfill Your Purpose

*#74 Is Your Life Unfolding Perfectly?*

*#80 Why Are You on Earth? SAGE Training*

*#105 Optimal Lifework*

**Books:** *Soul Proof, The Big Picture of Life*

**Audio Programs:** *Identify and Fulfill Your Purpose and Enjoy Your Greatest Life Technique*; *Pre-Birth Planning; Ask Your Soul, G.O.D. and Angels*

### Q#1: What are my current purposes for being on earth now?

A#1: That is one of the most important questions you can ask. The phrasing of your question suggests that you understand three important lessons:

1. Who you are is much more than your temporary earthly shell.

2. Your consciousness is visiting earth for important reasons.

3. Those reasons can vary over time.

Only you can answer your question, but I can suggest some guidelines for exploring those reasons. The articles and audio programs listed above have helped many people discover their missions. So has my SAGE acronym: *Service, Adventure, Growth, and Enjoyment*. Throw in *Love* for a comprehensive way to remember why people visit a place like earth.

In addition, I recommend answering the questions below from a deeply relaxed state of mind. This can be very helpful in learning / remembering why you are in this place at this time:

- What are you naturally good at?

- What would you do if money were no object?

- What would you do if you had only one year to live?

- In your youth, what did you want to be when you grow up?

- What do you read, search, and talk about in your spare time?

- What topics, thoughts, and visions do the following: choke you up, give you goose bumps, create tears in your eyes, and / or cause a mild pressure over your heart chakra?

I hope you enjoy the joy and peace from identifying and fulfilling your callings.

### Q#2: I thought only doctors and ministers had 'a calling'. Are you saying everyone has one?

A#2: I used to think the same thing but later realized that everyone has special reasons for being here. Each of those roles are important since **it's not so much what you do as how you do it**. A bus driver can be a powerful spiritual teacher by sharing smiles, kind words, and loving energies to everyone she meets. A quadriplegic can inspire others to tackle their comparatively minor challenges with style. Those who are very ill or disabled allow others to develop their care-giving abilities.

*Not all callings are easy, but all are invaluable.*

The more I ponder this, the more grateful I am about how life is set up. I trust how life unfolds and am in awe of how magnificent life is. I hope the same happens with you.

**Q#3: My husband died five years ago and it was very difficult for me. I decided to help others and regain a purpose for living, but none of it is working. The hospice program has too many volunteers and almost never calls me. The friends I helped ignored me once they didn't need my help anymore. Any suggestions?**

A#3: Serving others is a great way to make more sense in a world that seems senseless at times. However, I recommend that you leave the 'how to help others' more open-ended. You might better serve in another way that you haven't found yet. Drs. Bernie Siegel and Wayne Dyer told me, independently, that every day they asked Creator: "How can I serve?" Then they kept their senses alert and were patient. **That's a powerful two-step approach.**

Your soul's primary goal may be to develop patience and perseverance. If that is the case, you have a golden opportunity for that. How will you react now that your initial efforts didn't work out the way you wanted? You can't see the full picture of life right now so please don't judge your efforts to be a failure.

Michael Newton PhD, founder of *Life Between Lives(R)* sessions, had a client who described a previous lifetime. In it, her efforts to help others *seemed* to fail miserably. As she prepared to pass on, she thought that nothing had worked out. However, upon arriving to the next phase of life, she saw that *her so-called failures were actually preparation* for healing and counseling those who had been abused to death as children while on earth. The patience, perseverance, and skills she developed earlier helped her excel at this demanding task.

I hope that true story touches and helps you as deeply as it did me. From our limited human perspectives, we can't see the big picture of life. Our task is to feel for how we are called to serve and do that to the best of our abilities.

As for the friends who ignored you after they didn't need you any longer, that's not my definition of friend. See article #66 to learn how to develop more evolved relationships.

**Q#4: Is fulfilling my missions one reason why my soul wanted to come to a place like earth? It is so difficult here.**

A#4: Sharing your greatest gifts is a primary reason why people visit earth. They consider that to be worth the darkness that can make things seem so hopeless. Recently, I felt that I should watch the *Lord of the Rings* movies again. The fight scenes and violence are overdone, but I soon realized why I felt that urging. Each protagonist faced what seemed to be insurmountable odds **but didn't give up**. Working together, the heroes conquered formidable dark forces.

I know that life on this planet can feel VERY difficult at times. However, facing difficulties and overcoming adversity is a HUGE key to discovering who you are, why you are here, and living the greatest life of your dreams. Many people are awakening now. Collectively, we can turn this seeming trauma-drama into an exciting adventure with laughter, romance, and happy endings. Future generations can point to what we achieved and marvel.

However, much of life's apparent darkness and difficulties are self-generated. We create much pain and suffering via lower-energy thoughts, words, and actions. For example, when I experienced heartbreak after a first love breakup, I made things worse by repetitively thinking, saying, and acting as though the following were true: 'I'll never find another woman like her. My life will never be happy again. Why is life so cruel? I can't live without her.' *Not exactly an ideal recipe for finding the silver linings and improving my life.*

## IDENTIFY AND FULFILL YOUR PURPOSE

I could have thought, felt, and known: 'I wish that didn't happen, but I trust that an even better relationship is waiting for me at the right time and in the right way.' (It was.) Perhaps I needed to go through that largely self-inflicted pain to motivate me to find higher responses.

**What happens to us is much less important than how we choose to react to it.**

Many people would like their time on earth to be totally safe, fun, comfortable, and easy. But that's not why souls / people come to earth. They come here to love, learn, evolve, serve, and have adventures. Achieving those lofty goals can be difficult at times as you have experienced. However, the upsides are easily worth the pain and struggle, especially when you remember *'The Great News'*.

**Q#5: Isn't creating the greatest life of my dreams selfish? And what about people who think their greatest life is lots of alcohol, drugs, sex, and money? Is it OK for them to pursue that?**

A#5: You can optimally help the most people when you have the most wonderful life that YOU, as a soul / conscious being, have envisioned. Puritan ethics, that were interwoven in the early religious teachings of many people, made us fear anything that made us happy. But true happiness is the best compass to guide us toward how to live.

The following quote by Joseph Campbell is so wise and instructive that it bears repeating: "If you do follow your bliss, you put yourself on a kind of track that has been there all the while waiting for you, and the life you ought to be living is the one you are living… I say follow your bliss and don't be afraid."

Regarding your second question, many people have tried to find happiness with excess alcohol, drugs, materialism, sex, and other lower-energy pursuits. They may think that is the greatest life of their dreams and pursue it with gusto. Eventually, however, they discover that wasn't it. 'Eventually' may be several years or multiple lifetimes until they are willing to try higher paths.

# QUESTION SECTION #30: FOR MORE EVOLVED AND SENSITIVE PERSONS

Synonyms for the word *evolved* include: advanced, developed, higher, improved, progressive, and refined. Based on *Life Between Lives(R)* clinical research findings, Michael Newton PhD estimated that 15% of people currently living on earth have intermediate to advanced levels of consciousness / energies. That is another way of saying *15%ers* are more evolved people / souls. After working with many people for fifty years, it's clear that those who are more evolved are also often more sensitive and empathic.

The word *sensitive* is defined as: 'Quick to detect or respond to slight changes, signals, or influences.' *Empathic* is defined as: 'Identifying with the feelings, thoughts, or attitudes of others.' Both terms describe people who can sense more than the average human.

University-based scientific research has verified that some people can detect more of reality than usual. These heightened abilities may involve seeing, hearing, feeling, and / or knowing.

As you might imagine – or perhaps have personally experienced – it's not easy to see, hear, feel, and / or know more of reality than most people. At first, evolved / sensitive persons may think they are the only ones like that. Depending on religious, educational, cultural, and / or family factors, they may fear they are weird, possessed, or going crazy. Being in this minority can make a person *feel very different and alone at times.*

**Evolved / sensitive persons must take better care of their bodies / brains than 'average humans.'** The heightened and more sensitive energies of evolved persons require finer tuning of the body for optimal health and happiness. Without a purer and holistic lifestyle, symptoms and – over time – diseases can occur. Five decades of working in different healthcare fields with many people have helped me identify this connection. If you have read this far, you likely are a more evolved person. I am honored to share insights and resources. Please do the same with others who can benefit from the information.

## Articles

*#12 Holistically Fine Tuning Yourself*

*#23 Are You More Evolved and Sensitive / Empathic?*

*#32 Nutritional Based Healing*

*#56 Are You "The Weird One" In Your Family?*

*#87 Natural Health Care*

*#89 My Prayers*

*#100 Enlightenment*

*#101 When Reaching a Fork in Your Life's Road*

*#105 Optimal Lifework*

## For More Evolved and Sensitive Persons

**Books:** *Radiant Wellness, Greater Reality Living, The Big Picture of Life, The Eleven Questions*

**Audio Programs:** *Holistic Breathing; Life Review Technique; Past Life Regression; Pre-Birth Planning; Ask Your Soul, G.O.D. and Angels*

**Q#1: Covid, racism, riots, political division, economic concerns, etc. I can feel the pain and suffering of others and it's too much. I feel weird compared to others. Any suggestions?**

A#1: There is a good chance you are a sensitive / empathic person. As a result, you can sense the emotions and energy of others. You may feel their struggles and feel drawn to help them. However, you must shield and guard yourself so you can have a great life AND be a force for good / G.O.D. every day.

Remember when many people were excited about the year 2020? The beautiful metaphor of improving humanity's collective vision to 20/20 was certainly inspiring. Two years later, many people feel beat up, tired, and discouraged. I understand those feelings, but try to focus on:

- Things often seem darkest just before the dawn.

- Contrast is a powerful way to learn how you DON'T want to be.

- You can gain clearer vision by looking for and sharing the silver linings to life's clouds.

- Remaining strong and steadfast during adversity makes that easy and automatic during easier times.

- We volunteered for exactly this kind of experience. If not us, who? If not now, when?

- Strife can awaken sufficient numbers of people to make our world a better place.

- This brief earthly experience is a totally safe, meaningful, and magnificent adventure – a fleeting virtual reality experience – amidst forever. Deeply knowing that helps you to appreciate *and even enjoy* the journey.

Read the articles, take action steps, and use the audio programs listed for this section. That combination will help you share your strengths and stay balanced. **You are not weird, you are just different in a good way.** Many people on earth are in the genus-species *homo sapiens*, just one step beyond Cro-Magnon Man. While writing *Greater Reality Living*, Dr. Schwartz and I discussed a different classification for people with more evolved / advanced energies and ways of being: *homo evolvens*. We'll see if it catches on.

## Q#2: I find myself daydreaming a lot. Might that be an attempt to escape the bleakness of life on earth?

A#2: It could be. I saw a recent statistic that some people daydream nearly 50% of their waking hours. What a waste of precious time and mental energy! Excess daydreaming isn't a good long-term strategy for escaping *how it sometimes seems* on this planet. You can use your inner resources to make your life better and help others.

(I said *sometimes seems* because this earthly experience isn't the same for everyone. Some people, despite significant challenges, experience a heavenly life. Others, who have many blessings, describe it as hellish. You can choose the first perspective and enjoy a heavenly life all or nearly all of the time.)

Contemplation, in moderation, can be a positive practice that provides signs from your inner self about what to do next. Your inner musings may be reflections of remembrances from other times and places. Remember the powerful quote by Gandhi: 'Be the change that you wish to see in the world.' That doesn't mean you have to change the entire world for the better. Just start with yourself and those in your sphere of influence.

Meditation is a great way to quiet your brain so you can know within how to best live. A line from Rumi says this beautifully: "Secretly we spoke, that Wise One and me. I said, 'Tell me the secrets of the world.' He said 'Shhh, let silence tell you the secrets of the world.'"

Regarding your perception of how bleak life on earth can seem, remember that more evolved and sensitive people do best with optimal self-care, lifestyle habits, and natural healthcare. To learn more, see my book *Radiant Wellness: A Holistic Guide for Optimal Earthly Experiences*. Another key to focusing on all the good things about this planet is to 'find your tribe.' Meet kindred spirits who are more sensitive and aware like you. They can help you stay on the planet, do what you came here to do, and create the life of your dreams. (article #66)

**Q#3: I sometimes see shadows that move across the room or suddenly disappear when I turn to look at them. I see lights around people that vary in color from a brilliant beautiful white to pinks and greens. None of this frightens me, I just don't know why it happens.**

A#3: You may have a form of extrasensory perception (ESP) that involves clairvoyant or "clear seeing" abilities. This allows you to see more of the 99% of reality that escapes the senses of many people. Another way to describe this is that you may see *energy fields or auras*. The 'shadows' may be postmaterial people or other beings who are there.

More ethereal visual images disappearing when a person turns to look at them is commonly reported. Why? When catching an image with your peripheral vision, the brain isn't fully engaged in judging whether that perception is 'really real' or not. When you look directly at them, your analytical brain – and its programming from your earth-training indoctrination – concludes 'There is nothing really there'.

Put another way, brain-induced filtration can reduce sensing the greater reality. It's adaptive to not hear all the sounds, see all the images, and feel all the sensations that exist around us. We couldn't function optimally if we could. But **expanding your perceptions just a bit can reveal more of what is and help you remember your true nature and missions.**

Appreciate your special experiences and share them with others who will support you. More people now report expanded perceptions of life. Training to extend your senses is available through the following people I know or know of: Suzanne Giesemann, Janet Nohavec, Susanne Wilson, and Kay Reynolds.

**Q#4: I am very sensitive and that makes it tricky to participate fully in this world. Part of me really doesn't want to be on this planet. What can I do to get more grounded, fulfill my missions, and enjoy this earth journey?**

A#4: Thanks for your candor and stating those goals so clearly. I had to smile when I read your note. In my early twenties, I thought there had to be a mistake that I was living on earth. While hiking in nature, I raised my arms up and yelled toward the sky: 'Beam me up, Scotty. There's been a mistake!' Over time,

I realized that I could enjoy a heavenly state of being no matter whether I'm on this planet or elsewhere. *Approaches for fulfilling your goals...*

1. Read the articles and use the audio programs listed above, especially *Holistic Breathing*.

2. *Optimize your body / brain* with prayer, meditation, yoga, time in nature, and other centering practices. (article #77)

3. Regularly exercise, eat a whole food diet, rest, and use other tips in *Radiant Wellness*.

4. Each day, **express gratitude** for all the love, support, and assistance you receive from your higher-energy assistants and The One. Affirm that you are always shielded, guided, protected, centered, and balanced. Envision being surrounded with a cocoon of love and light so you aren't sapped or zapped by people with lower energies.

5. *Enjoy time with kindred spirits* at open-minded and open-hearted spiritual centers. Activities that draw awakening people include: meditation, dances of universal peace, music, chanting, drumming, service outreaches, and holistic workshops.

6. *Learn more about the nature of reality* and how to embrace it fully. (My favorite website for this is SoulProof.com, but I might be a little biased.)

7. *Serve others.* Helping others creates an opportunity for sacred alchemy as you transmute lower-energy emotions and ways of being into higher ones.

**Q#5: I wonder if we sensitive people have more attachment to objects? When my living space is a mess, my**

**body gets tired more easily and seems to soak up negative energy. I also seem to draw people to me who are struggling with fears and problems.**

A#5: Sensitive people may gather more clutter because they:

1. Value objects from the past, especially those from loved one.

2. May not be organized due to their extrasensory perceptions and otherworldly interests.

3. Require an optimal balance between body / brain and spirit, but don't know about or address that. Over time, this may cause fatigue, depression, anxiety, obesity, and other symptoms that make it more difficult to manage their home and life.

*Your observation about sensitive people being drawn to those who are struggling is* **spot-on**. Many advanced souls / people on earth choose jobs that help others. However, some people in need may not be ready to change. As such, trying to help them can be frustrating and deenergizing. Imbalanced people who are struggling may try to gain more energy by *sapping* – stealing someone's chi – or *zapping* – trying to feel better temporarily by lashing out at others. In either case, it can diminish the sensitive person who is trying to help.

It took me a long time to realize that my job is to do my very best as I teach, heal, and help others. Then I need to *disengage and not take on responsibility for someone else*. It's not my business whether they listen and follow through, or not. Who knows what their souls' agendas might be for this earthly visit. They may need to hit rock bottom before they awaken to their self-sabotaging actions. Or they may have volunteered to be mentally and / or physically ill so others could improve their diagnostic and care-giving skills.

**Q#6: I am looking for advice for my eight-year-old son who has a gift of sensing spirits. He's scared to death to be alone. His experiences started before he was three: spirits contacting him and sometimes feeling them inside of him. We've saged our house, prayed a lot, told "it" to leave, and had a pastor come pray. But nothing has worked. My husband's family has several gifted members so sensing spirits does run in the family. I'm dying for his fears to go away so our family can become normal again.**

A#6: Your son is lucky to have such a wise and caring mom. Seeing more of the greater reality – including postmaterial persons – is a gift that can seem difficult initially. I know a number of top-rated mediums who describe how scary it was for them at first. Now they help many people in powerful ways.

I would keep it low key, provide lots of support, and let him be a kid as much as possible. Attend enlightened places like Unity and Spiritualist Centers. Attend drumming, dancing, and chanting groups in your area. He may be shy at first, but will likely love being around others who have higher energies and recognize the primacy of consciousness. Relaxing massage and acupuncture can release tenseness from his muscles and optimize energy flow.

When the topic of sensing spirits comes up, talk about it openly, briefly, and reassuringly. If possible, ask your husband's sensorily-gifted family members to talk with your son. Tell him a story about a little boy who had special gifts and learned how to handle them. Use the shielding methods discussed in article #23.

Pray to The Light and higher-energy assistants to protect him from *imbalanced entities* (so-called 'evil spirits') and *interim PMPs* (ghosts). In the name of love and Light, instruct 'spirits' to not scare him, wake him, or enter his body. Balanced PMPs will honor those requests and boundaries. Imbalanced beings cannot overcome the power of love and light. When your son is older and ready, teach him more about these beings. (articles #47 and 104)

Watch TV and online shows about mediums with him so he learns that he's not the only one. Watch *Harry Potter* and other fun movies about children with special powers. Cats, dogs, and horses – who may perceive more of reality than the average material person – can be a great source of comfort and kinship.

In my opinion, he doesn't have a problem that needs fixed. He has a special gift that needs nurtured so he can develop it and help others. As he gets older, ensure that he doesn't turn to alcohol and / or drugs – whether illegal or prescription – to numb his perceptions and cope in self-defeating ways.

Regarding your sentence *'I'm dying for his fears to go away'*, he may pick up on your energy. Please use prayer, time in nature, and meditation *for yourself and other family members* so higher energies of peace, hope, joy, love, and gratitude predominate in your home.

# QUESTION SECTION #31: RELEASING OLD WOUNDS, FEARS, AND MISINFORMATION

Cruelty, prejudice, physical harm, ridicule, rejection, and other lower-energy behaviors are so common on this planet. Many people have been abused emotionally, physically, and / or sexually. All this CAN result in significant emotional, mental, and physical wounds.

Many people have been taught false information about Creator, life, death, and afterlife. You know the list of these fearful teachings that have haunted and hobbled so many people: life ends after bodily death; you are a lowly and helpless sinner; there in only one way to salvation; you could end up burning in hell forever; etc. All this CAN result in fear and ignorance.

**Or all that CAN motivate you to rise above it**: heal old wounds, release needless fears, and learn evidence-based information. This will allow you to evolve, create a great life, help others, and make our world a better place.

That's why I capitalized the word CAN. You can choose to reach the higher ground, to find and share the blessings – no matter what has happened or is happening to you.

Ancient spiritual teachings addressed this opportunity via metaphors that speak to people throughout the ages. Here's one of my favorites:

> You are like an ornately decorated and precious golden bowl. Pure white light, love, and energy always reside within and can shine out from this vessel. However, that light may be *partially or totally blocked* by accumulated debris from pain, fear, sadness, ignorance, and old wounds. Your mission is to clear that out so you and others can see your true brilliance and benefit from it.

Powerful, safe, and time-tested methods exist to release old wounds, fears, and limiting teachings. There are many aspects to these **soul-utions**, thus the long list of articles and resources. I am honored to share these with you.

## Articles

*#10 Optimally Handling Life's Biggest Changes and Challenges*

*#11 Expanding Your View of Life*

*#12 Holistically Fine Tuning Yourself*

*#19 Great News to Remember During Your Earthly Experience*

*#29 Suffering: Optimally Handling Life's Changes and Challenges*

*#40 The Love, Acceptance, and Forgiveness Technique*

*#46 Unforgivable Sin?*

*#49 When You Have Been Abused: How to Heal and Transform*

*#50 Choosing Action Over Discouragement*

## Releasing Old Wounds, Fears, and Misinformation

*#51 Meditation and Relaxation Techniques*

*#52 All Life Is Interconnected*

*#58 It's Just a Game: Optimally Handling Life's Biggest Challenges*

*#61 When a Relationship Breaks Up*

*#65 Karma*

*#66 Optimal Relationships for Evolved People*

*#67 Contrast Souls*

*#70 Holistic Breathing Technique*

*#71 Ask Your Soul, G. O.D. and Angels*

*#74 Is Your Life Unfolding Perfectly?*

*#77 Centering Practices*

*#84 Heal and Transform Your Suffering Technique*

*#86 Breathing Techniques*

*#91 Pause and Remember*

*#100 Enlightenment*

*#101 When Reaching a Fork in Your Life's Road*

**Books:** *Soul Proof, Greater Reality Living, Radiant Wellness, The Big Picture of Life, The Eleven Questions*

**Audio Programs:** *Holistic Breathing; Life Review; Heal and Transform Your Suffering; Pre-Birth Planning; Love, Acceptance, and Forgiveness; A.R.T.; Ask Your Soul, G.O.D. and Angels*

**Q#1: Personal relationships throughout my life have been filled with emotional, physical, and sexual abuse. I'm 54 and live by myself with five cats. I just pray that my life after death is better than this one. I'm no longer in ANY relationships and am even estranged from my so-called family. Why do other people have soulmates and love, but I don't?**

A#1: Space didn't allow me to list all the abuse you've encountered. You'd be surprised how often I get letters like this so you're not alone. No one could or should blame you if you remained stuck in bitterness, hurt, isolation, etc. for the rest of this earthly experience. However, your reaching out suggests that you are interested in finding the upsides. It's likely that you are an evolved and sensitive person, thus your: (1) difficulty in relating with 'average' humans, (2) challenges in reaching a balance in your life, and (3) love of furry spirits.

Wise teachers ranging from the Buddha to Vince Lombardi have been quoted as saying, *'Fall down seven times, get up eight.'* Those words describe how you can choose to react to adversity. (Another great quote by Coach Lombardi: 'Perfection is not attainable but if we chase perfection, we can catch excellence.')

Like many people, you may love books, movies, and plays in which the protagonist overcomes seemingly insurmountable odds. Why? Because those stories remind you of a common reason that people visit earth: *to remember and demonstrate in a challenging environment how wise, special, and powerful you are.* The *Star Wars* series is a great example of how much people are inspired by adventures.

## Releasing Old Wounds, Fears, and Misinformation

The words of Princess Leia have become immortalized: 'Help me, Obi-Wan Kenobi! You're my only hope.' Actually, however, *there is always hope and each of us can be heroes.* Realizing this enables you to take the high road no matter what is happening to you or around you. Joseph Campbell taught this ultra-important lesson in his books *The Hero's Journey* and *An Open Life*.

Remembering who you are and shining brightly in this sometimes dense and difficult place builds strength of spirit. Common sayings capture this vision: *the strongest metals have gone through the hottest fires,* and *that which doesn't kill me can make me stronger.*

There are a number of reasons why you may have chosen to endure such abuse:

    1. *You have / are an evolved consciousness* who volunteered to let people with imbalanced and immature energies to experience – now or during their life review – to *see, feel, and know* the ripples of their negative actions. As a result, they will hopefully do better from here on. (article #100)

    2. *You may embody intermediate energies* and want to grow and serve more. You knew that the abuse *could* – not necessarily would since it depends on how you react – achieve that.

    3. *You may be a beginner soul* who chose to go through all this because you abused others in another time and place. This **karmic boomerang effect** isn't retribution, it's an opening for deeply learning how to treat yourself and others. (article #65)

Holistic methods can help you transmute your pain and sadness into joy, peace, meaning, and empowerment. It's a sacred process of alchemy that is easier and more possible than you might imagine. To start with, I recommend changing your focus FROM 'Why do other people have soulmates and love, but I don't?' TO 'How can I develop wonderful and loving soulmate relationships?'

**As always, focus on what you want, not what you don't want.**

If you choose to take the path with heart, you will need to make changes and you will need allies. **Here's how I would start if it were my adventure.** And, although it may not seem that way to you, this relatively illusory earthly / virtual reality experience is an exciting adventure.

1. Read the free articles listed above and take appropriate action steps. There are a lot of them, but you have gone through much abuse and difficulty. *Having a breakthrough instead of a breakdown will require a multifaceted approach.* Make a few changes at a time and pace yourself. You can journey FROM where you are now TO where you want to be.

2. Listen to my free radio interviews as I and top experts discuss why there is so much suffering and what you can do about it.

3. Use the very affordable audio products listed above. Start with *Holistic Breathing* to release old wounds, negative emotions, etc. Let yourself cry, yell, pound the mattress, and massage tight muscle areas that may store lower energies.

4. Ponder whether you may have unconsciously blocked great people from your life because you can't handle another rejection. When you feel ready, give one or two of the best candidates another chance.

5. Read article #66 and use the four-step formula for finding optimal relationships.

Over time, these steps can help you open to and attract others so you can enjoy healthy and loving relationships. You deserve those and the world needs your highest self.

**Q#2: Could prolonged abuse as a child cause feelings of being separated from life and a Higher Power? I have struggled all my life with this. It causes great fear and unease.**

A#2: Yes, being chronically abused can cause a *dissociative shift* in which you distance yourself from people and life in an attempt to prevent further hurt. From an energetic perspective, turning off your circuit breakers can perhaps prevent further pain. Your unconscious intention may be to protect and numb yourself in an attempt to survive. That was perhaps your best option as a child, but now you have other better ones.

You've obviously matured and processed some of this since you are reaching out for guidance. You now have an opportunity to live the greatest life you have imagined and feel the joy that comes from personal relationships with others and Source. **You can enjoy life fully and bless others, not in spite of your abuse, but because of it.** You didn't give up and now you have special gifts and inner strength to share.

My recommendations for you are the same as those listed above. May you soon feel the bliss of knowing you are an integral, eternal, and precious part of All That Is *now*.

**Q#3: Mark, I feel caught in fear after a series of events: I was sexually abused as a child; my parents had a violent divorce; I was moved from relative to relative; my father died by suicide; I was in a mental hospital; one of our children died; my wife and I got divorced; another child was diagnosed with a brain tumor. I'm feeling really overwhelmed and would love some wise guidance.**

A#3: Wow! That's quite a list, but it's not the record. Now you know why I say that *only the bravest and / or most bullheaded people volunteer to attend earth-school.* You may be very strong, visionary, and / or impulsive to have chosen so many difficulties to work through. As you now know, many powerful benefits await your mastery of those challenges. Holistic methods can help you journey through the toughest situations and fulfill your reasons for being on earth.

Use my recommendations listed throughout this book. Your recovery will take some although it may be much less than you think. It's quite likely that you can become a more peaceful, happy, and energetic person after 9 months of addressing this holistically.

Here are two excellent quotes that I would post where you can see them often…

> *'Keep your face always toward the sunshine, and shadows will fall behind you.'*
> – Walt Whitman

> *'We must let go of the life we have planned to accept the one that is waiting for us.'*
> – Joseph Campbell

**Q#4: I was deeply in love with a woman and, although she rejected me, I still miss and think about her a lot. I'm sure she was 'the one true love' for me. If I can reunite with loved ones after I die, is that possible with her?**

A#4: Oh my, *unrequited love* – the subject of so many poems, songs, books, and movies. It hurts so bad and seems so unfair. After I 'lost' my first love, I awakened with my pillow wet from crying in my sleep. I had fleeting thoughts of suicide to end the severe pain and sadness. I know exactly what you're going through and have worked with others who experienced a similar heartbreak. You are not alone, my friend.

## Releasing Old Wounds, Fears, and Misinformation

However, life isn't so unfair and limited that there is just 'the one true love' for you. I'm living proof of that. Many blessings for you and others await IF you can move beyond the sadness, loneliness, anger, etc. In my case, that breakup was a major factor in awakening to the greater reality at a young age. *The old me died in a way.* That felt scary and painful but motivated me to ask important questions and seek sensible answers. That likely wouldn't have happened if I married my high school sweetheart. My current relationship is a quantum leap better.

How to start? One of the wisest pieces of advice I've ever heard is: *Always reach for the highest feeling thought.* During my deepest pain, a thought that helped me was, 'At least I may get to see her in heaven someday.' The same is true for you.

For how long and in what way you might see her is secondary. Just knowing that you and she – and everyone else – are sacredly interconnected can provide the peace and meaning you seek. If that break-up rocked your world so much, you two may have interacted before in another part of The Field of All Possibilities. You might be surprised to find her in the welcoming line after your body dies. That may especially be the case IF you take the high road between now and then.

*Love is an energy, a level of consciousness.* You can experience love within and all around even when you seem to be alone. Your feelings of love seemed to be tied to her but, actually, she was just a reminder of your true nature. She was a catalyst, a mirror, who helped you get in touch with who and what you really are. *It can be very tough at first to move beyond the messenger and focus on the message that **love is all there is**.* To increasingly 'grok' that, use the recommendations for all questions in this section.

Love is something you can give to yourself and everyone you meet. It's a level of awareness that upgrades every aspect of your life. Whether the love you feel is returned by a certain person or not is very secondary in importance. All the love you put out comes back to you; it transforms who and how you are, and thus benefits all those around you. Your energy, light, and love are what you take with you wherever you are.

It's difficult, or maybe impossible, to experience real love with another without a certain level of *self-love*. Some people who don't have that yet seek to fill their inner void with another. They project in their minds what that person is and can't see the real person. That's why it's smart to wait about two years in a relationship before concluding that you have met an optimal match for you. It often takes that long to discover who and how the other person really is.

Perhaps she is a primary soulmate and you two designed this potentially heartbreaking scenario. Why would you do that? To push you to search for meaningful answers to life's biggest questions. To remember who you are and live accordingly. To have an opportunity to transmute your pain into loving service and the greatest life you have envisioned. I hope your heartbreak rekindles loving relationships with yourself, The One, and everyone you meet.

# Question Section #32: Natural Health Care for Common Imbalances

Many people suffer with a multitude of symptoms, syndromes, and named diseases. This has gotten significantly worse – especially with young people – since I first started working in health care fields fifty years ago. A tsunami of physical and mental symptoms was predicted in the 1940s after well-run experiments with cats directed by Francis Pottenger MD.

Dr. Pottenger fed the following to two groups of cats: raw milk and meat OR cooked and devitalized food. His prediction was that the second group would develop an array of mental and physical symptoms. That started by the second generation and was so severe by the third generation that the research was halted. The list of symptoms is exactly what many people are experiencing now, especially young people. Prescription drugs and surgery can't help when nutritional deficiencies, lack of enzymes, and abnormal flora are the culprits.

Royal Lee DDS and Weston Price DDS were two other early pioneers in the field of whole food nutrition and supplements. Why two dentists? A clear link between good nutrition and dental health had been identified by then.

Many naturally oriented health care providers today consider those three to be legends. But most doctors who use only drugs and surgery have never heard of them. In the 1930's, much of the food supply shifted FROM fresh and local sources TO processed and shipped foods from agribusiness and food industries. Since then, every generation has increasingly suffered from that and other factors listed below:

> topsoil depletion; overcooked and over-processed food; excess junk foods, sugar, and artificial sweeteners; chemicals sprayed on crops, given to animals, or added during processing; excess alcohol and illegal drug use; insufficient exercise; excess stress; unwise prescription drug use, especially excess vaccinations, antibiotics, and painkillers; over-stimulation via excess TV, digital games, computer use, and porn; inadequate parental supervision and prudent discipline; lack of meaningful teaching about Creator and the nature of reality.

These underlying causes of common physical and mental symptoms were listed before. But it's so important that you and others know them and react wisely. The good news? Common health problems that predictably occur due to these factors can often be prevented and reversed with optimal self-care, healthy lifestyle choices, and natural healing methods.

## Articles
*#12 Holistically Fine Tuning Yourself*

*#26 Holistic Solutions for 'Mental' Symptoms*

*#30 Spirituality and Porn*

*#32 Nutritional Based Healing*

*#33 Six Stressors*

*#37 Detoxing Chemicals and Heavy Metals*

#38 Holistic Solutions for Common Symptoms

#43 Dirty Electricity and What You Can Do About It

#51 Meditation and Relaxation Techniques

#54 The 90 Day Program to More Energy, Clarity, and Fitness

#57 Immunity Enhancement Program

#64 Drugs, Alcohol, and Greater Reality Living

#77 Centering Practices

#86 Breathing Techniques

#87 Natural Health Care

#88 Whole Food Way of Eating and Supplements

#89 My Prayers

#90 What Do I Eat?

**Books:** Radiant Wellness, Greater Reality Living

**Audio Programs:** Holistic Breathing; Ask Your Soul, G.O.D. and Angels

***Q#1: I am depressed and terrified of dying. My anxiety about death makes everything seem pointless; I am tired emotionally and can't enjoy life. I know the afterlife evidence, but it doesn't seem real. I hope you can help me.***

A#1: *What you are experiencing is **your body / brain telling you that something is out of balance**.* Similar symptoms have been helped many times with *a personalized holistic healing program* that addresses the root causes. Your body can heal itself; it just needs some help to remove interferences to that process. You've likely forgotten how great it feels to be happy, energetic, and healthy. My recommendations to getting well again include:

1. Assemble a holistic support team: integrative medical doctor, nutritional practitioner, chiropractor, acupuncturist, and minister / counselor. Chronic feelings like yours pose a risk of suicide; please tell close family and friends about how you've been feeling and let them help.

2. Read the articles listed above and the *Radiant Wellness* book, then take incremental action steps. The time, energy, and money required to do this will be eminently worthwhile.

3. Remember that your energy / consciousness is what you take with you when you pass on. After getting fine-tuned, you'll be able to help others by your presence and example.

4. Use the *Ask Your Soul, G.O.D. and Angels* technique to obtain guidance about how to optimally move forward.

5. Be patient; people who go to health care providers are called patients because it takes time to heal.

After your body and brain are working better, revisit the collective afterlife evidence in articles #1 and 60. Read *Greater Reality Living* for strategies to internalize that evidence and *'The Great News'* so that informs and empowers your time on earth.

**Q#2: I've consulted you for over three years and am doing much better. As you know, I used to have a horrible drug and alcohol addiction. I am free of all that after your help, counseling, and other approaches. I am thinking**

*about just drinking wine moderately. I'm very aware of what alcohol did to me in the past but, if I feel changed, shouldn't I know what works for me?*

A#2: Given your severe history of drug and alcohol use, I definitely WOULD NOT try to drink wine in moderation. Why risk it? It's normal to want to feel happy and good, but alcohol is a horrible way to do that for addicts. Even for a non-alcoholic, drinking bacteria urine – which is what alcohol is – is an inferior buzz. There are better ways to *get high and stay high* instead of coming down and risking injury, illness, and addiction.

I used some alcohol, pot, and a few magic mushrooms in my twenties. But I wouldn't do any of that if I could it do over again. Instead, I would use: yoga, meditation, time in nature, great music, higher thought classes, optimal self-care, natural health care, inspirational books, services at different religious / spiritual centers, loving relationships, serving others, fulfilling my highest missions, and enjoying time with evolved persons. That approach has increasingly helped me feel energetic, happy, and peaceful over the years.

My favorite 'mind expanding' substances these days are green tea, dark chocolate, and rotating different mushroom tea powders: chaga, reishi, cordyceps, and lion's mane.

You're at a fork in the road about drinking and can learn the hard way or the easy way. You've already suffered immensely via the drug and alcohol route. Perhaps you should listen to someone with my training, experience, and track record in helping others?

**Q#3: *I suffer with a long list of symptoms: migraines, depression, insomnia, fatigue, brain fog, high blood sugar, anxiety, OCD, high blood pressure, skin rashes, constipation, and more. I think my medical doctors***

***wonder if I'm crazy. I used to take ten medications but felt worse. I've heard about natural care, but can that really help problems like mine?***

A#3: Often times, yes, IF you do your part in getting well again. I've seen your symptom list and worse many times over the last 37 years of working as a holistic physician who uses spinal adjustments and nutritional healing. Many people suffer with these and other symptoms. It's a clear sign of how well the disease-care approach to health is working. Medications, as you discovered, often make things worse and don't address underlying causes of the symptoms.

If you are ready for a better way, follow my guidelines in A#1. Getting well again will initially require time and money but less as you improve. Many years ago, hand operated pumps raised water up from a well. To get the water coming out of the spout required a lot of pumping. But after it was flowing, it just required an occasional movement of the handle to keep it going.

You are in a hole, so to speak, with your health and energy. After your vitality is flowing again, it will require less care and money to *stay well*. In the long run, you will save time and money. More importantly, you'll feel great again and be able to share your greatest gifts.

A patient I'll call Audrey came to me at age 65 with a longer list of symptoms than yours. I recommended chiropractic, nutrition, and improved lifestyle habits. It was slow going at first, but month by month she felt, looked, and acted better. After about nine months of care, she came into the treatment room crying. I thought she had gotten worse and asked why she was crying. 'These are tears of joy', she said. 'I feel so good now. *I had forgotten what happy felt like.'* I hope you do what it takes to feel happy again too.

*Q#4: I want to improve my diet and way of living but feel worse when I try. It's especially hard to give up sugar, coffee, cigarettes, and junk food. I get more headaches and feel more fatigued. What can you recommend?*

A#4: Many people are similarly addicted to stimulating substances that you listed. You didn't mention it, but you likely spend too much time watching TV, using the Internet, playing electronic games, and / or watching porn. Typical signs are a shorter attention span, and repetitively shaking an arm or leg.

*Excess sugar, caffeine, nicotine, and chemicals in junk food contribute to your symptoms.* They each have the potential to become addictive; the more you use, the more you want. That's one reason people who know better don't use those substances that act as *neuroexcitins and neurotoxins.* Drs. Michael and Mary Eades state that white sugar, white flour, and other additives in junk food can stimulate the brain like cocaine. Those substances rev up the brain for a while and then you want more. Unless you escape this vicious cycle, it's just a matter of time before you develop even worse physical and mental symptoms.

Follow the recommendations outlined in A#1 of this section. In addition, incorporate *centering practices* into your daily lifestyle. These will help you calm down, quiet your brain, and break your addiction to stimulants. There's a long list of ways to do this so pick a few that sound best to you and get started. (article #77)

# Question Section #33: Optimal Relationships for More Evolved People

High-level relationships are very important for *more evolved people* who manifest / are intermediate to advanced energies. As they awaken, they usually desire a spiritual path and kindred spirits. This section was especially designed for these *15%ers*. By contrast, less evolved people – AKA *average earthlings* – may be beginner souls. I don't use the term 'average earthling' in a judgmental or critical way; that's just their stage of development and / or functioning. They have lower-energy emotions and ways of being *at this time*, but that can always improve.

How can you identify more evolved persons? They tend to question and search for sensible answers instead of blindly accepting traditional ones. More advanced people focus on what will create more peace, joy, love, gratitude, fulfillment, service, and enlightenment for them and others. They tend to be less materialistic or, if they do have very nice things, aren't overly attached to them. They are less egotistical, more altruistic, and often are teachers and healers. In general, their interests and preferences reflect their evolved energies.

Earthly experiences of more evolved people flow better when they *optimally fine-tune every aspect of their lives*: self-care, lifestyle habits, life work, leisure activities, **and relationships.** That includes relationships with family, friends, co-workers, and – if desired – a significant other. When evolved persons don't have those needs met, they may suffer disproportionately compared to those whose lower energies aren't so affected.

## Articles
*#53 When You Encounter Loss*

*#56 Are You "The Weird One" In Your Family?*

*#61 When a Relationship Breaks Up*

*#66 Optimal Relationships for Evolved People*

*#67 Contrast Souls*

*#71 Ask Your Soul, G. O.D. and Angels Technique*

*#74 Is Your Life Unfolding Perfectly?*

*#101 When Reaching a Fork in Your Life's Road*

**Books:** *Radiant Wellness, Soul Proof*

**Audio Programs:** *Holistic Breathing; Pre-Birth Planning; Past Life Regression; Life Review; A.R.T.; Love, Acceptance, and Forgiveness; Ask Your Soul, G.O.D. and Angels*

**Q#1: I've had a series of relationships that start well, but then don't work out. What is really important to me isn't to many people including possible mates. How can I find a partner who is interested in the topics you write about?**

A#2: Many people, including myself, have gone through the same learning curve. In general, the more awakened you become, the better it is when your partner / spouse is also. Younger persons often have lower-energy focuses: Good looking? Money and a good job? Pleasant personality and shared interests? Those are all important, especially as a young adult when sex, having children, getting a nice house, and career advancement are priorities.

However, more evolved persons ALSO need to focus on a spiritual path, the journey of awakening, and service to others. This may be especially true as they enter their middle and senior years. Finding other members of your tribe / soul group is an important key to having optimal relationships.

Read the articles listed above and use audio products that seem useful for you. Become a vibrational match for what you want using this formula:

1. Pray, intend, and affirm that you receive assistance and guidance in this process.

2. Write everything you would like in a relationship with friends, family, and – if and when you are ready – a significant other. Don't hold back, the sky is the limit. Don't let your brain get in the way and incorrectly judge what is possible for you.

3. Fine-tune yourself holistically so you are *an energetic match* for the relationships you want. For example, if you want to meet people who regularly meditate, do yoga, and help others, then do that yourself.

4. Stay alert for what I call *lovable characters* – people with whom you have a rapid, happy, and mutual connection.

5. Frequent places where more evolved and sensitive persons go. Your list may vary, but here is where I've found more evolved persons to congregate:

a. Unity Centers; Centers for Spiritual Living; Unitarian Universalist churches; Sufi, Buddhist and Hindu centers; Spiritualist churches; Native American and shamanic spirituality groups

b. Churches with an open-hearted, open-minded, and service-oriented focus.

c. Holistic health centers, classes, and retreats

d. Centers / classes for meditation, yoga, drum circles, kirtan, sound healing, and dance

*Being your real and best self* is a big key to developing optimal relationships. When you live in alignment with who you really are, you express your uniqueness and special nature. That's a great way to find *people who like you, and not waste time with those who don't*. Being your authentic self puts you in the flow of life and attracts others who are a great match.

**Q#2: My wife passed on three years ago and I am totally alone. I considered her to be my soulmate. Any ideas about how I can meet other kindred spirits?**

A#2: Follow the same recommendations listed in A#1. In addition, know that you are really never alone. Believing that you are alone keeps you in lower-energy emotions such as sadness, fatigue, and hopelessness. You don't want to attract new relationships from that level.

Your angels, guides, master teachers, and others are present to assist, guide, and comfort you. This can especially be the case when you ask for it, give thanks, and use it to bless others. Use the extra time to improve yourself and attract better relationships of all types when the time is right. Remember that **appearing to be alone does not require you to feel lonely**. As you increasingly like and love yourself, you'll enjoy your own company more and so will others.

You have a golden opportunity to expand your relationships and maybe even find a new primary one. Use the *Ask Your Soul, G.O.D. and Angels* sessions to check in with your inner guidance about how to optimally move forward. Grief groups with higher functioning people may help. In the future, Greater Reality Living groups will be available online and in person. (To learn more, visit SoulPhone.com/Greater Reality Living.)

**Q#3: Shouldn't some early counseling steer us toward optimal relationships instead of learning by trial and error?**

A#3: Wouldn't that be great? Or would it? Maybe the searching and subsequent learning is part of the process. Perhaps evolved relationship counseling will be available someday via postmaterial counselors using SoulPhone technology. Until then, use the recommendations listed above and be your authentic self. Don't hide your interest in spirituality, higher thought, and afterlife topics. Trust your inner heart and mind to find those who share your passions.

Some gay people try to 'stay in the closet' and hide their sexual orientation. They try to be happy with a heterosexual relationship and 'pass' as a straight person. Over time, however, a significant percentage of these relationships fail and many people get hurt. In the short and long run, everyone would be better off by living their highest truths. Similarly, more evolved people can benefit by coming out of 'the spiritual closet', following their interests, and finding their tribe.

**Q#4: Can improving my relationship with Creator also help my relationships on earth?**

*A#4:* I made this the very last question in this book because it is such an excellent one. *Perceived or actual abandonment issues with people* can cause feelings of unworthiness that block optimal relationships. In addition, *feeling alienated from Source* can negatively color your beliefs about deserving earthly relationships. So, yes, having an excellent relationship with your Higher Power is very important for enjoying ideal relationships with family members, friends, and significant other(s).

# Afterword

Ten years ago, I began awakening after a long and deep night's sleep. I was at that stage of 'What time is it? What day is it?' Then I became aware of what seemed like a very important sentence that had been repeating itself over and over in my mind. I wanted to catch it, so I closed my eyes and breathed deeply. Then I wrote it down so I wouldn't forget. Here it is...

**'This earthly experience is a totally safe, meaningful, and magnificent adventure amidst eternity.'**

That is one of the most concise and wise statements about life on earth that I've ever heard. I can't take credit for it since it may have come from E.L. G.O.D. and / or my higher-energy assistants.

You are in eternity now. That can seem heavenly or hellish depending on a number of factors discussed in this book. I hope that you take time to understand and internalize this. You deserve to enjoy the greatest life of your dreams and fulfill your highest reasons for being on earth. And the world is just waiting for you to share your greatest gifts.

Just before sending this book to the publisher, I finished *The Lord of the Rings* third movie. As mentioned, I had felt that I should watch them for some reason. While facing seemingly hopeless odds against superior numbers of dark forces, the lovable dwarf

## Afterword

warrior Gimli uttered this classic line: "Certainty of death? Small chance of success? What are we waiting for?"

His courage and resolve in that situation were admirable. However, we on earth in 2022 have it much better than that. A more accurate and hopeful statement is: **'No one really dies. We have every chance of success. What are we waiting for?'**

It's true since death is an illusion since only a small fraction of who and what we are perishes. And *we have eternity* to accomplish and enjoy all our goals, dreams, and missions. So what are we waiting for? I hope my paraphrase of Gimli's epic statement helps you remember how very powerful, special, and capable you are. Sharing your greatest gifts and being your highest self provides an important piece to solving the puzzle of harmony and love on earth.

**And here's a fun fact** that makes this point even more impactful. Gimli **appeared** to be very short compared to the other human and elven warriors. *However, in reality,* the actor playing Gimli was, at 6 foot 1 inches, *the tallest of all the actors*. He **seemed** so short, right? His scenes were shot on a different stage with cameras closer to him so he looked shorter. Those images were superimposed upon the others to complete the effect. A 4 foot 1 inch tall stunt double – kind of a parallel reality version of Gimli – completed the illusion.

I was 'over the moon' when I read about this because it's such a perfect metaphor for how *seeming appearances* on earth prevent us from seeing more of the greater reality.

I'll end this book as I started it, with a list of *'The Great News'*. These statements are based upon the collective scientific, clinical, and firsthand experience evidence about life, death, and afterlife. Based upon the existing clinical and scientific knowledge, very high degree of certainty exists that these statements are true. In addition, many people know that these statements are true based upon their personal experiences and inner knowing.

Knowing *'The Great News'* is so vital for making sense of this earthly experience, completing your missions, creating the greatest life of your dreams, and making our world a better place. This news can help you – no matter what is going on around you – to live with peace, joy, love, gratitude, compassion, meaning, enthusiasm, enlightenment, and other higher-energy emotions / ways of being.

### *'The Great News'*

The collective evidence indicates, with high degrees of certainty, that *you and everyone else:*

1. continue to live after bodily death, and may be living in parallel realities now.

2. do not really lose 'departed' loved ones and can interact with them again.

3. are integral, infinite, eternal, and beloved parts of Source Energy / Creator.

4. receive assistance / guidance from angels, guides, master teachers, and evolved energies.

5. are sacredly interconnected with all people, animals, and nature.

6. have special purposes for being on this planet at this time.

7. have everything you need to survive and even thrive during this earthly adventure.

## Afterword

8. possess a magnificent body that, when cared for, can optimize your earthly experience.

9. can find meaning and trust the timing behind life's biggest changes such as death.

10. co-create how heavenly / hellish your life feels by your thoughts, words and deeds.

11. can find silver linings and opportunities for growth and service amidst challenges.

12. can likely use SoulPhone technology in the future for communication with postmaterial loved ones and luminaries who can help us heal our world.

My dream message, comments, and *'The Great News'* say so much that anything else would be redundant.

**May you always deeply know and show who you are, why you're here, and Who walks beside you. May you fulfill your highest callings and enjoy the greatest life you have envisioned.**

# Glossary

**N**ote: I use single quotation marks around terms that don't, in the light of contemporary evidence and understandings, have fully accurate meanings. Examples include 'death', 'departed', and 'deceased.' Some of these terms won't be familiar since I – with and without collaboration from Dr. Gary Schwartz – 'coined' or created them. Those terms will be designated with an asterisk.

Admittedly, new and modified terms require some time and effort to incorporate into your vocabulary. However, *upgrading the words you use while thinking and speaking can enhance your beliefs and resultant actions.* Newer and more accurate terms can assist a deeper knowing of *'The Great News'* and expand your degree of greater reality living.

***15%er*** is a term to describe the approximate percentage of *people on earth at this time who have intermediate to advanced energies.* Calling them *evolved souls* is another way to describe this group. The term 'old souls' isn't accurate since energy advancement is the result of evolution / awakening, not how many years a soul / person has existed. If you are reading this book, you may be in this *15%er* group that holds great hope for many people and our planet.

**After Death Communication** (ADC) describes a meaningful perception, while awake or dreaming, of postmaterial loved ones. (article #28)

## Glossary

***A-Team*** refers to thirty postmaterial luminaries who have assisted the research and development of the SoulPhone Project. This term is worth learning since these 'deceased' geniuses may one day assist positive transformation on our planet.

***Awaken*** is used synonymously with become enlightened, see the Light, perceive more of the greater reality, attain realization, see life's bigger picture, and have a spiritually transformative experience. All these terms describe the process of 'really getting' that there is much more to life than meets the eye.

***Awareness***: see Consciousness

***Bereaved / Shining Light*** describes how very sad and grieving bereaved people can increasingly realize that their postmaterial loved one is now a *shining light*. PMPs enjoy – or soon will be – very high levels of love, peace, joy, enthusiasm, clarity, and much more. *They want their dear ones on earth to do the same now* and also become shining lights. (article #82)

***Centering practices*** is a term for different ways to *quiet the brain and glimpse more of the greater reality*. The brain detects less than 1% of what exists. Material persons suffer in so many ways when guided solely by this limited brain that insists its perceptions are all that exists. Centering practices help you to regularly and deeply be still and know you are an integral part of creation. (articles #51, 77, 86, 89, 91)

***Change Worlds:*** see Death of Earthly Body

***Cross Over:*** see Death of Earthly Body

***Channeling*** is what an extrasensorily gifted person does by relaying information from higher energies: angels, guides, master teachers, and / or a collective of higher consciousnesses.

***Consciousness*** is that which perceives and experiences events before, during and after an earthly incarnation. For simplicity, I will use the word consciousness synonymously with *mind* and *awareness*. These terms describe *that which exists before human birth, animates the earthly form, and continues living after death of the earthly body.*

**'*Death/Die*'** are heavily anchored to meanings that your 'departed' loved ones have ceased to exist, are rotting in the ground, have been reduced to ashes, or are very far away. Other beliefs reinforced by these limiting words are that you may never see these dear ones again, or you can't communicate with them until you pass on. Much contemporary evidence indicates that none of these beliefs are true. I will instead use terms listed under *death of earthly body*.

**Death of Earthly Body** is a term used to indicate a vitally important distinction. **YOU** do not die, just your no-longer-needed earthly form does. The earthly vehicle that takes you from womb to tomb has been discarded but your energy / consciousness / awareness continues to exist. Similar terms include: *body dies, death of human form, earthly body dies, and death of your earth-suit.* These more accurate terms help you remember that the vast majority of who and what you are survives after your earth-suit perishes.

**'*Deceased / Departed*'** historically referred to people after their earthly bodies die. These words may be misconstrued in ways listed under 'Death and Die'. I will use more cumbersome but accurate terms such as: 'Your dear one who is in the next phase of life' or 'Your postmaterial loved one'.

**'*Devil*'** is a word used by conservative religious denominations in a few religions to describe a supposed formidable embodiment of evil that can thwart Creator's plans. The idea of a literal 'devil' was never seriously considered by mainstream theologians or most denominations.

**Earthly Experience** describes your brief time on earth. Your life existed before your human birth and continues after your earthly form dies. Thus, saying 'this life' while referring to your time on earth can be confusing. Since your knowledge and consciousness shape how you perceive reality, the term *earthly experience* also acknowledges that each person's adventures while visiting earth are unique. This term also opens the door for the possibility / probability of multilocation AKA parallel realities or simultaneous existences.

Finally, the term earthly experience reminds us that – contrary to what human senses commonly report – we aren't solid, physical, and separate people who eventually die. Our consciousness is 'just visiting' this planet for a short while in a way that may be very much like a brief virtual reality experience.

\***E.L.G.O.D.** stands for the Energizing, Loving, Guiding, Organizing and Designing presence and power in life. A shorter version of this is G.O.D. The Creator and Sustainer of All Life has historically been called many names. Synonyms include: Life Source, Higher Power, The Light, All That Is, One Mind, Unitive Consciousness, and others listed in the Dedication. *El or Al* – the root words of Elohim, Eloha, Allah, and other sacred names for Unitive Consciousness – meant *The One* or *That One* which expresses itself uniquely through all things.

**Energetic Body AKA Astral or Spiritual Body**, refers to the historical energy system of a person that exists before human birth and continues after the earthly body dies. In his book *The Living Energy Universe*, Dr. Schwartz refers to this as an *info-energy system*. This energetic body may manifest in apparent physical form depending on the intentions and observer. For example, postmaterial persons may be perceived as having physical form when visiting humans, greeting recently 'deceased' loved ones, or enjoying various activities.

**Energy** describes the power and vitality of a person or system. In discussions about consciousness, the word energy refers to *that which cannot be destroyed*. Recognized by various cultures, this life-force is also termed chi, ki, prana, bioenergy, and innate intelligence.

**Evidential Mediums** are people with *extrasensory / sensitive abilities* that exceed the normal range of human perception. These can involve clairaudience (clear hearing), clairvoyance (clear seeing), clairsentience (clear feeling), or claircognizance (clear knowing.) Mediums usually convey messages from postmaterial loved ones, but others specialize in teaching and research.

**'Evil Spirit'** see Imbalanced Entity

**Field of All Possibilities** is a term for 'where you go' after your earthly body dies. However, it's important to realize that *you and everyone else are in that field right now* – it isn't just somewhere you go after leaving earth. All life exists in a field including our earthly experiences now. Synonyms include: afterlife realms, the next phase of life, different spacetime scenario, and other planes of consciousness. More religious / spiritual terms include Heaven, Home, and the Really Real Place.

**Fine-tuning your body / brain** is so important for an optimal earthly experience. It's very difficult to know, let alone show, how wonderfully life is set up when you're tired, depressed, anxious, fearful, and / or suffering with one or more major imbalances. The degree to which you sense how magnificent life really is depends on how well your hormonal, nervous, immune, and gastrointestinal systems are working.

**Force** has a standard definition of energy or power as the result of physical action. Some after death communications involve alterations in electronic device functioning or movement of physical objects. As such, I consider that force can be produced by post-material persons and higher-energy assistants just as it can by material persons.

**'Ghost'** has strongly engrained meanings of a stuck and distraught dead person who can hurt you, but better understandings exist now. I will use the term *interim PMP* for those persons who, for a variety of reasons, may not enter the Light immediately after bodily death. (#47)

**'God'** is a term that often conjures up images of a huge dictatorial man who sits on a throne in the sky. Wars have been fought and millions tortured and killed over whose is the one true 'God'. As such, many people are ready to move on from this millennia-old patriarchal image and word. The term 'God' is also strongly tied to the Judeo-Christian religion. In my usage, 'God' is used when referring to archaic and erroneous images of Creator.

**Greater Reality** describes *the totality of life*. Most of this is not perceived by the average material person. Different people – mediums, shamans, mystics, and other more *sensorily-gifted* persons – can perceive more of the fullness of life. Synonyms include: all that exists, absolute reality, and the big picture of life. (article #72)

**Greater Reality Living** is a term that invites you to consider how you might live, and treat others and our planet, as you comprehend more of life's bigger picture. What higher-energy paths might you take when you deeply know *'The Great News'*? What changes when you deeply know that bodily death is a relatively minor event in the bigger scheme of things?

**'Heaven / Hell'** are topics that sorely need reexamined given original and contemporary understandings. Some people considered them to be physical places where people live after bodily death. The former is way up in the sky where that giant long-haired guy who runs everything lives. The latter is far below the earth's crust. (You'll know you're getting close when you see a huge red guy with horns.)

*Actually, the terms 'heaven and hell' originally meant* **how you feel and how life seems** *given your degree of love and state of consciousness.* They are primarily degrees of awareness that *E.L.G.O.D. is all and is in all.* A hellish life – whether living on earth or elsewhere – is self-induced and temporary. A heavenly life is always an open-ended possibility for you.

Alternate terms for where / how part of your life force can live after bodily death include: *the really place, the afterlife, the next phase of life, the field of all possibilities, and a different realm.* Another synonym is *Home* which is capitalized to differentiate it from the house you live in. (article #14)

**Higher-Energy Assistants / Assistance** – from a religious / spiritual viewpoint – describes angels, guides, master teachers, and other evolved beings. (The term 'master teachers' refers to spiritual teachers around whom religions formed and others of that level.) From a secular perspective, this can be seen as *Higher-Energy Assistance*. (articles #13 and 73)

**Higher-Energy Emotions** include love, peace, joy, compassion, gratitude, enthusiasm, hope, acceptance, and enlightenment. *Consciously focusing on these higher energies and ways of being* is vital for a meaningful and totally successful earthly experience. *Lower-energy emotions* include hatred, guilt, fear, anger, hopelessness, revenge, self-blame, and excessive grief. When focused upon too much, these can engender poor choices, illness, self-destruction, and other negative results that you don't want in your life.

*Feelings / emotions – and their underlying energies – have huge consequences.* They shape your view of reality now and after you change worlds. For example, feeling angry a lot increases the intensity and frequency of angry thoughts and words. Over time, that can result in lower-energy actions toward yourself and others. Collective lower-energies of humanity are considered to be one cause of extreme weather, violence, and other disasters on our planet. To learn more, read *Power Versus Force* by David Hawkins MD, PhD.

**Holistic** refers to understandings or solutions for what has historically been termed *body, mind, and spirit*. However, I propose upgrading that phrase. The word 'body' is OK, but I often use the term body / brain since they are so interdependent. For example, the GI tract can produce as many neurotransmitters as the brain; an imbalanced nervous system can impair functioning of the GI system.

However, 'mind' is problematic since it is used synonymously with awareness and consciousness by scientists and clinicians in survival of consciousness fields. 'Spirit' has varying meanings for different people. As such, I propose *body, brain, and consciousness.* The meaning of each word is more precise and widely agreed upon. Using *brain* in this phrase also emphasizes the role that organ plays in perceiving reality and communicating with the transcendent source of awareness.

**Human Birth** is a term that recognizes that YOU existed *before* your earthly body formed. Adding *human* to the word *birth* highlights that your outer form is just *a tiny fraction of who and what you really are.*

**Information** is a term describing *data or facts* that are learned or conveyed. The field of *systems theory* – as taught by Dr. Ervin Laszlo, author of *Science and the Akashic Field*, and others – holds that reality can best be understood as the totality of energy and information stored in a quantum void. Dr. Schwartz combines energy and information in his concept of *dynamical info-energy systems*.

A number of factors determine whether your awareness of this info-energy results in experiencing being on earth, a different time-space possibility, or perhaps an undifferentiated unitive state. Further, in this view, expanded access to energy and information is possible under certain conditions. One example is the commonly reported enhancement of perceptions after a spiritually transformative experience. Different cultures and disciplines have described the repository of this info-energy as Akashic Records, Hall of Truth, or Collective Unconscious.

**\*Imbalanced Entity** is a term I designed to replace 'evil spirit.' Just as there are immature and malicious material persons on earth, the same appears to be true in other planes of existence. The term *imbalanced entity* describes immature and chaotic manifestations of energy.

**\*Interim Postmaterial Person**, an alternative term for 'ghost', refers to those whose earthly bodies have died, but haven't moved into the Light. Part of their energy / being is still on or near earth instead of another realm. (article #104)

**Karma** is a principle noted by some religions, philosophies, and clinical evidence. A *cosmic boomerang effect* has been described as, 'You get back what you put out' and 'You reap what you sow'. Belief in this presumption encourages us to intend, think, speak, and act in higher-energy ways since those shape what we experience.

**Level of Energy / Soul Development**: people / souls may be basically categorized as *beginner, intermediate, or advanced*. These terms are not judgmental and do not imply a hierarchy of better or worse. In afterlife realms, it is widely understood that all beings are important and sacred reflections of the One. However, not all people know and show that equally, thus the need for terminology that describes the current stage of realization.

These descriptions have been used by Michael Newton PhD and others to describe where a person / soul is in their current development. David Hawkins MD, PhD measured those energies and described them in his book *Power Versus Force*. As such, there are at least some objective measures behind these terms.

**'Lose / Loss / Lost'** will not be used when referring to a loved one whose earthly body has died. *It may seem as though* you really lost them, but much evidence shows this is not the case. If you haven't seen, heard, or felt their presence, know that some *sensorily-gifted people can*. You might think your loved ones are lost and gone forever when, in fact, they are literally tapping you on the shoulder.

**\*Material Person** describes a person who is usually described as 'human', 'those living on earth', or 'earthling'. Why create a new term? *Material person* contrasts nicely with *postmaterial person* (PMP), an upgraded term for those whose earthly bodies have died. Those terms emphasize that – except for the earthly body – postmaterial persons share many similarities with material persons.

*Understanding the nature of* material persons / humans is a prerequisite for internalizing *'The Great News'*. You *appear* to be only a physical person who ages, dies, and ceases to exist after bodily death. But, actually, you're a timeless being of awareness / energy, and much more than your five senses report. (article # 15)

**Matter** refers to a solid substance as compared to energy. In physics, matter is considered to occupy space and contain mass at rest whereas energy does not. However, electron microscopes reveal that matter is not as solid as it might appear. Matter consists mostly of empty space. Perceptions of matter – whether it appears solid or not – depends on *who is observing*. Regarding the nature of matter and energy, quantum / electro-dynamical physics holds that they shift back and forth many times per nano-second with accompanying particle and wave characteristics.

The shifting appearance and nature of matter and energy provide key insights for more fully understanding the nature of reality. It may assist comprehension that material persons are relatively illusory manifestations of energy. From 'a particle perspective', solid and separate persons appear to be living on earth for a while until they die. However, from 'a wave perspective', material persons may be best understood as beings of energy who can appear solidly, or not, depending on who is observing. For now, please consider that matter may not be as solid, nor energy as insubstantial, as you may have believed.

***Mind***: see Consciousness

***Multilocation*** is also known as *parallel realities* or *simultaneous experiences*. These terms describe the possibility that YOU – your essence / energy / consciousness / mind – can experience more than one time-space aspect of life simultaneously. For example, part of YOU may manifest as a person on earth, another part as a formless being in another realm, and part that never leaves The One. All this can perhaps be best viewed as *a series of virtual reality experiences* – relatively illusory, but as real as life on earth seems. This topic can be a bit of a mind bender so see article #75 to learn more.

***Near Death Experience*** (NDE) describes perceptions a person may have while clinically dead. NDEs have been independently described very similarly across time and in various cultures. Blind people and children have reported *documented NDEs*: accurate observations of events that a clinically dead person could not sense unless, indeed, consciousness exists independently of brain function.

## Glossary

**'Nonphysical Being'** and similar terms – *discarnate, unseen being, formless entity,* and *disembodied being* – are based on what the average material person's senses can detect. However, some material persons can sense PMPs so that isn't a good guideline for terms. So-called 'nonphysical beings' may be just as, or even more, physical and solid compared to those living on earth. As such, I avoid these terms unless accompanied by single quotation marks.

**Out of Body Experience** (OBE) refers to a person's awareness leaving the body without being nearly dead. This can occur spontaneously, in meditative states, and during intense situations such as childbirth or imminent danger. OBEs can also be facilitated by techniques designed for that purpose. These experiences provide *personally meaningful firsthand evidence* that consciousness exists independently of the brain. There are also some documented aspects of OBEs as authenticated by researchers, for example, at The Monroe Institute.

**Perinatal Experience** is an awareness – recalled spontaneously or during hypnosis – of the time period just before, during, or after human birth. Perinatal experiences usually involve young children who accurately describe specific details about events during those time frames. This has been documented many times even though the children had never been told about those events. Research about this phenomenon by physicians and psychologists further indicates that awareness pre-exists and operates independently of the human brain.

**Person** is a term that usually describes someone living on earth. The term 'soul', on the other hand, has historically been used to describe a person after bodily death. However, contemporary evidence indicates that *much about a person persists after the earthly form dies*. Memory, intelligence, preferences, sense of humor, love, and much more continue to exist. I will use the word 'person' to denote a material person. When referring to a postmaterial person, I will use that term or alternately, person / soul or person / consciousness.

***Postmaterial Person** (PMP) refers to so-called 'dead, deceased' and departed' persons. This term recognizes that *the great majority of who and what you are continues to live after your no-longer-needed body perishes*. Put another way, this term describes those whose earthly body have died, but are yet very much alive. Good evidence indicates that PMPs can manifest in physical form depending on their intentions and with whom they are interacting.

Even though their earthly form has perished, PMPs are *still human* in meaningful ways. For example, they can appear in a familiar earthly guise when working with researchers. They also retain human qualities and abilities developed while living on earth. PMPs can also visit earth or stay there for extended periods of time. As such, they are or can live on earth. Finally, the term 'earthling' is too anchored to discussions about aliens who say: 'Greetings, earthlings. Take us to your leader.'

I hope the acronym PMP will be commonly used along with NDE (near death experience), ADC (after death communication), and STE (spiritually transformative experience). (article #31)

**'Reincarnation'** is a term mistakenly associated with cults or the occult. As such, it can negatively trigger those with conservative religious beliefs and / or who are uninformed about the topic. The word also typically denotes experiencing life in chronological order while in different bodies on earth. Since this view is overly simplistic, I will instead use terms listed under Multilocation. This usage also acknowledges the evidence that linear time is only relatively real. As such, the past, present, and future may paradoxically coexist. (article #34)

**'Soul'** is a commonly used term with little actual agreement about its meaning. Ask ten people who aren't in the same religious denomination to define 'soul' and you'll understand my motivation for upgrading this term. 'Soul' is also well-anchored to images of a fleeting and gauzy dead person who can fly around. This notion is based more on archaic beliefs and typical human perceptions than contemporary evidence. Research indicates that PMPs are not so ethereal and can manifest physically when they want / need to. For these reasons, I often use the word 'soul' with another, for example, soul / person.

**Soulmate** refers to persons with whom you have had close connections in different spacetime experiences. These kindred spirits may help during your visits to earth, greet you after your earthly body dies, and help you learn and grow. Michael Newton PhD, founder of the *Life Between Lives* technique, stated that we each have twenty-five or so primary soulmates and a larger number of secondary and tertiary ones. The existence of soulmates is also reported by evidential mediums, near death experiencers, and spiritual traditions.

**'Spirit'** is used synonymously with 'soul' by some people. Capitalized, it also can describe Creator, especially as Great Spirit. However, the word 'spirit' may mistakenly convey something to be feared, particularly when paired with the adjectives *evil or ghostly*. As with soul, spirit has connotations of a life form that is fleeting or insubstantial. For these reasons, 'spirit' isn't a term I'll use much.

**Spiritual** is a term with varying meanings. Dictionary definitions focus on *relating to spirit, soul, or sacred matters*. *Spiritual* can also describe more open-minded considerations of ultimate matters as opposed to orthodox religious views. I will use this word – and its related forms spiritually and spirituality – since those are so well established in our language. Examples include: spiritually transformative experience, spiritual center, and evolved spirituality.

***Spiritually Transformative Experience (STE)*** describes a deeper knowing about the big picture of life. As with NDEs, STEs can engender a more humanistic viewpoint and cause people to reorder their priorities. STEs can be triggered by the bodily death of a loved one, NDE, OBE, ADC, childbirth, exposure to violence, meditation, consciousness altering drugs, deep love and other causes. (article #17)

***'The Great News'*** is a term to describe twelve inspiring and comforting pieces of information about the nature of reality. The collective scientific and clinical research about life, death, and afterlife indicate that these twelve points are quite probably true based on very high degrees of certainty. That term is both italicized and included in single quotation marks to clearly label this list.

**YOU** in the capitalized form conveys a person's total energy and being. Put another way, 'you' describes who most people on earth think they are, while YOU connotates who they really are. I will sprinkle the term YOU throughout the book as a teaching tool to remind you that who you are is much more than your earthly body and brain-generated thoughts.

# Resources

This section provides Information about Dr. Pitstick's FREE articles, radio shows, and newsletters. It also reviews his books and audio programs so you can learn which resources and products might optimally help you.

## Articles
*Over 100 free articles* with holistic solutions for the most common challenges while on earth. SoulProof.com/Articles

## Radio Shows
Twenty *free radio interviews* with top experts in the fields of afterlife, consciousness, and optimal living. Guests include (in alphabetical order): Mark Anthony, PMH Atwater, Wayne Dyer, Stan Grof, Bill Guggenheim, Neil Douglas-Klotz, Jeffrey Mishlove, Raymond Moody, Anita Moorjani, Caroline Myss, Michael Newton, Ken Ring, Bernie Siegel, Marilyn Schlitz, Gary Schwartz, Brian Weiss, and Karen Wyatt. SoulProof.com/Radio Shows

## Newsletters
*Free monthly newsletters* with answers to recent questions, SoulPhone Project updates, and information about upcoming webinars and other opportunities. Sign up at SoulProof.com and SoulPhone.com

## Books
*Ask the Soul Doctor* Holistic answers to the most commonly asked questions about the toughest parts of this earthly experience.

*Greater Reality Living* Collective evidence for 'The Great News' and how that can enhance how you treat yourself, others, and our planet.

*Radiant Wellness* A holistic guide for optimal wellness so you can enjoy the greatest life YOU have envisioned.

*Soul Proof* Compelling evidence that life continues after bodily death and the benefits of really knowing and showing that.

*The Afterlife Evidence* A concise and clear review of the scientific, clinical, and firsthand experience evidence that clearly indicates continuation of consciousness after bodily death.

*The Big Picture of Life* (targeted to ages 10 – 16) Answers to life's biggest questions such as 'Who am I? Why am I here? What happens after I die? Is there really a Higher Power?' and more.

*The Eleven Questions* Answers from top consciousness experts about everything you ever wanted to know about life, death, and afterlife.

## Audio Products
(Note: Products #1 – 4 and 6 – 10 involve deep relaxation / hypnosis)

1. *A.R.T. Technique* Achieve higher levels of Appreciation, Realization, and Transformation about all 'losses' in your life. Learn to *reach for the highest feeling thought* no matter what has happened or is happening to you.

2. *Ask Your Soul, G.O.D. and Angels* Access wise guidance from your higher self, The One, and higher-energy assistants about how to improve every area of your life.

3. *Facilitated After Death Contact* (Facilitated ADC) Expand your awareness of postmaterial loved ones and enjoy a wonderful and meaningful relationship with them now.

4. *Heal and Transform Your Suffering* See past and current sufferings in a new light to benefit from the blessings that always accompany them.

5. *Holistic Breathing* Release trauma, heal emotional wounds and regain stuck energy for full potential living. Uses deep, noisy, diaphragmatic breathing with music and coaching in the background. Used across time and cultures to expand consciousness and assist healing.

6. *Identify and Fulfill Your Soul's Missions AND Create the Greatest Life of Your Dreams* The long title is self-explanatory.

7. *Love, Acceptance, and Forgiveness Technique* No matter what happened in the past, you benefit by Loving, Accepting, and Forgiving yourself and others. Free up energy by releasing hatred, denial, anger, and other lower-energy emotions.

8. *Life Review* If *your body died* today, what would your life review be like? Find out, then make amends and improvements so your life review after you pass on will be *a work of art*.

9. *Past Life Regression* Visit other time / space scenarios that YOU may have dreamed up / experienced. Release old traumas to heal chronic physical and mental symptoms. This technique can also allow you to explore parallel realities/ simultaneous experiences.

10. *Pre-Birth Planning: Did I REALLY Plan All This?* Recall if and why you may have chosen the possibility of certain events – especially perplexing and challenging ones –during this earthly experience. Revisit the time / place of your life planning with assistance from your angels, guides, and the Light.

# About Dr. Mark Pitstick

Mark Pitstick, MA, DC, has fifty years of experience helping people in hospitals, pastoral counseling settings, mental health centers and holistic health care practice.

His training includes: bachelor of science degree in zoology (Ohio State University 1975); graduate theology studies majoring in pastoral counseling (Methodist Theological School of Ohio 1977 – 1978); master of arts in clinical psychology (Western Carolina University 1980); and doctorate in chiropractic health care (Palmer College of Chiropractic 1985). Mark has completed extensive postgraduate training in clinical nutrition. While attending theology school, he provided suicide prevention counseling and education.

When Mark was six years old, he told his parents that a beautiful sunset 'reminds me of God.' Mark became aware of occasional clairaudient and clairsentient abilities at age ten; he's had a number of miracles, revelatory, and spiritually transformative experiences.

After working in hospitals with many suffering and dying adults and children, he was motivated to find evidence-based answers to questions that many people ask: "Who am I? Why am I here? What happens after I die? Will I see my departed loved ones again? Is there a God? If so, why is there so much suffering? and How can I best live during this brief earthly experience?"

## About Dr. Mark Pitstick

Dr. Pitstick wrote the books *Soul Proof, Radiant Wellness, The Eleven Questions, The Afterlife Evidence,* and *Ask the Soul Doctor* with endorsements from Drs. Wayne Dyer, Elisabeth Kubler-Ross, Deepak Chopra, Bernie Siegel, and others. He also co-authored Greater Reality Living (with Gary E. Schwartz PhD), and The Big Picture of Life (with Dr. Schwartz and Katta Mapes MA, MEd).

Mark produced the *Soul Proof* documentary film with interviews of people who had near-death experiences, after-death communications, and other eye-opening encounters. His eleven audio products use deep relaxation, breathing techniques, and guided imagery to help people deeply *know and show* they are integral, infinite, eternal, and beloved parts of Source. He created the Ask Your Soul, Your Life Review, and Facilitated ADC techniques.

A frequent media guest, Mark hosted *Soul-utions*, a radio show about practical spirituality, and *Ask the Soul Doctors* with interviews of top consciousness experts. His interviews with Brian Weiss MD, Caroline Myss MA, Michael Newton PhD, Anita Moorjani, and others can be heard at Radio Shows. He has given many workshops / webinars on spiritual awareness and holistic wellness.

Pitstick is certified in past life regression therapy by Brian Weiss MD, and the psychomanteum technique by Raymond Moody PhD, MD. Mark was the executive vice-president of Eternea started by Eben Alexander MD and John Audette MA. Mark provides clinical support for Helping Parents Heal group leaders and *Caring Listeners*, and contributes to their newsletter for bereaved parents.

Mark directs the SoulPhone Foundation that: (1.) teaches the collective evidence for life after death to people worldwide, and (2.) supports 'spirit' communication technology research and development at the University of Arizona. He is a research assistant for the SoulPhone Project at their *Laboratory for Advances in Consciousness and Health*.

As of 2020, data from seven controlled experiments has *definitively demonstrated scientifically* that life does not end after bodily death. Further, this research has demonstrated reliable communication with postmaterial (so-called 'deceased') persons. These studies have met the criteria for true scientific research: double-blinded, multicentered, experimentally controlled, replicated, randomized order, and published in peer-reviewed scientific journals.

Mark founded Greater Reality Living groups to help people prepare for the paradigm shift after official announcements and public demonstrations in 2022 – 2023 of scientific proof of life after death. These announcements and public demonstrations will occur after completion of multicenter studies and development of an optimal SoulSwitch. To learn more about Dr. Pitstick's outreaches, visit SoulProof.com and the above websites.

www.ingramcontent.com/pod-product-compliance
Lightning Source LLC
Chambersburg PA
CBHW071650090426
42738CB00009B/1474